T4-ADN-548

Maybe It Happened *This* Way

BIBLE STORIES REIMAGINED

Rabbi Leah Rachel Berkowitz
and Erica Wovsaniker

Illustrated by
Katherine Messenger

For Amma, the next chapter in our story.
—RLB

For my Grandma Sally, who would be so proud of me.
—EW

For my parents, who first told me stories.
—KM

Apples & Honey Press
An Imprint of Behrman House Publishers
Millburn, New Jersey 07041
www.applesandhoneypress.com

ISBN 978-1-68115-586-9

Text copyright © 2022 by Leah Berkowitz and Erica Wovsaniker
Illustrations copyright © 2022 by Behrman House

All rights reserved. No part of this publication may be translated, reproduced, stored in a retrieval system or transmitted, in any form or by any means, electronic, mechanical, photocopying, recording or otherwise, for any purpose, without express written permission from the publishers.

Library of Congress Control Number: 2022936204

Design by Katherine Messenger
Edited by Dena Neusner and Leslie Kimmelman
Editorial consultant: Debra Hirsch Corman
Printed in the United States of America

1 3 5 7 9 8 6 4 2

"Ben Bag Bag said:
Turn it, turn it, and turn it again
for everything is in it.
Look at it closely, grow old reading it;
And do not move away from it,
for there is no better gift."

—*Pirkei Avot* 5:22

Contents

What Is Midrash?   vii

Introduction: Maybe It Happened This Way   1

CHAPTER 1 · Adam and Eve Grow Up   5

CHAPTER 2 · Noah's Hope   17

CHAPTER 3 · Go Forth and Smash the Idols!   25

CHAPTER 4 · Rebecca Goes Forth   33

CHAPTER 5 · Sisters Stick Together   47

CHAPTER 6 · Standing at the Edge of the Pit   55

CHAPTER 7 · A Matter of Life and Death   67

CHAPTER 8 · Miriam Saves Her Brother   75

CHAPTER 9 · Moses Sees   87

CHAPTER 10	·	Dancing on the Shores of the Sea	95
CHAPTER 11	·	Standing, Sitting, and Signing at Sinai	103
CHAPTER 12	·	(Don't) Give Up Your Gold!	111
CHAPTER 13	·	Follow That Goat!	121
CHAPTER 14	·	Please, God, Heal Her	129
CHAPTER 15	·	Seeing through Caleb Eyes	137
CHAPTER 16	·	Moses Turns Away	149
CHAPTER 17	·	Why Curse When You Can Bless?	157
CHAPTER 18	·	Sisters Stand Up for Justice	169
CHAPTER 19	·	The Remembering Song	177
CHAPTER 20	·	The Crowns on the Letters	185

Discussion Guide   191
- Values Guide   192
- Discussion Questions   197
- Index of Values and Sources   204

Acknowledgments   207

What Is Midrash?

SOME OF THE STORIES YOU WILL READ IN THIS BOOK MIGHT feel familiar to you. Some stories—or parts of stories—will feel entirely new. You might ask, *Hey, are you making that up?* And the simple answer is, *Yes, yes we are.* We had a lot of fun using our imaginations to create new stories about familiar characters—or even to invent new characters to add to familiar stories—so that we might find new meaning in a very old book.

Did you ever try to make up an explanation for a plot hole in your favorite series? Or wonder what two characters from different universes might say to each other if they met? There have been generations of people who have asked those same kinds of questions about the Torah.

The stories we create when we use our imagination to add new layers to Bible stories are called midrash, from a Hebrew word that means "to search or explore." And we aren't the only ones who do it. People have been creating midrash pretty much since the Torah was written. Midrash may attempt to explain something in a passage that doesn't make sense or help us understand why certain characters do what they do. Midrash may be intended to teach a lesson about something important. Or midrash may be designed simply to entertain, the same way we write fan fiction about our favorite book and movie characters.

We believe that the best midrash does all of the above. And it usually starts with a question: Who? What? When? Where? Why? How?

The stories in this book include pieces of the original story from the Torah, bits of traditional midrash from the generations before us and from creative people we know, and interpretations that came from our own imaginations. The traditional sources we've used can be found on pages 206–208. (If you are a teacher, you may want to bookmark that section!)

Do you know what the best thing is about midrash? You can do it too! If you want to imagine what a character in the Torah is feeling or thinking, what happens after a story ends, or what happened before it started, we hope you will take out your preferred tools—pencils or paints, fabric or clay, laptop, dancing shoes, or musical instruments—and make some midrash of your own!

INTRODUCTION

Maybe It Happened This Way

MAYBE, IN THE BEGINNING, THERE WAS CHAOS AND VOID, *tohu vavohu*, and then God spoke, "Let there be light," *y'hi or*, and there was light. Then light was separated from dark, then the skies and the waters and the land were all separated from each other, like piles of laundry. God gave order to the light and the dark, the sun and the moon and the stars, days and nights and months and seasons. Then the skies and the waters and the land were filled with life, soaring life and swimming life and creeping and crawling life, scaled and feathered and hairy life. Days went by, one, two, three, four, and five, and all of Creation was good. Finally, on the sixth day appeared the less hairy but excessively large-brained creatures, in their varied forms. These God called very good, *tov m'od*. Six days to go from nothing to everything. Then a day to rest.

Or maybe there was nothing—void—and then there was a big bang. Chaos. Then the chaos swirled itself into order, over centuries, millennia, eons. Big rocks became spheres; spheres fell in line around giant balls of gas; other spheres and other balls of gas lined up this way and that. And, eventually, one of those rocky spheres—at least one, maybe more—saw life appear. Maybe that life started off as barely noticeable, as specks and motes. Then those specks and motes organized themselves, made creatures bigger than themselves, in which some of the specks were for breathing and eating, and some of the motes were for hearing and seeing, and thus living things that could walk, could talk, could love and laugh and think came into being.

Maybe that big bang and God's *ruach*—spirit, or breath—are one and the same. Maybe the day on which light was separated from dark and the day on which the creeping and the crawling and the hairy were created were in fact eons apart.

Or maybe when God wanted to create the universe, God already took up all the space there was. So as God created, God stuffed Godself in a vessel, like a clay pot, to make room for the world. But the more God created, the more of Godself had to be stuffed in the pot. Eventually, just as God was putting the finishing touches on Creation, the overstuffed vessel exploded, sending pieces of God, as well as pieces of itself, all over the universe. And it's our job to find those pieces of God from behind those pieces of the vessel and bring them back together again, thus repairing the world, *tikun olam*.

Maybe before there were any creeping or crawling or hairy creatures, God's own hands molded a being out of clay—*Adam*, from *adamah*, "earth." Only then did God make all the things that crept and swam and soared, and only then, when none of those things turned out to be a suitable counterpart and companion for *Adam*, God sculpted an *isha*, a woman, from *Adam*'s rib, and they became *ish* and *isha*, "man" and "woman."

Maybe all of these stories are true. Maybe more than one truth can exist at the same time. Maybe we need one truth sometimes and one truth at other times. What's important is not necessarily finding the answers. What's important is continuing to ask the questions, to take these ancient stories and turn them over and over again, learning new truths and asking new questions.

CHAPTER ONE

Adam and Eve Grow Up

She opened her eyes and saw a big smile and an outstretched hand.

A sound issued from the smile. "Hi. I'm Adam. Let me show you around the Garden of Eden."

So she took Adam's hand and followed him.

There was an abundance of everything in this garden. A sparkling blue river weaved through vibrant green ferns and teemed with fish in every hue of sunlight. Tall trees stood on the banks, with fruits of every size, scent, and description. Every once in a while, Adam would pluck one of these fruits and hand it to her, and they all were juicy and sweet and yet different from each other—a rainbow of flavors.

"There's one tree we can't eat from," Adam told her. "It's in the middle. I'll show you." He led her down the banks of the river.

As they walked, the garden turned into something more like a forest—thicker, greener, and noisier. "What are those sounds?"

Adam tilted his head and listened. "Those tweet-tweets are birds. I named them." He sounded proud of himself, which made her smile. "And that rustling—well, it could be a bunch of different animals. A horse. A mouse. A wolf. We'll see all the animals eventually; I'll show you which is which." He thought for another moment. "If the rustling is sort of quiet and subtle, that's the Serpent. We aren't supposed to talk to him."

"Why not?"

"We just aren't." He kept walking.

She kept walking, too, but continued her questions. "Why is that great big light in the sky moving?"

"It's the sun. It goes across the garden in the day, then at night it disappears, and a bunch of smaller lights appear. Well, one sort of medium-sized light and a bunch of smaller ones."

"Why?"

"They just do."

"How do the fruits we eat appear on the trees and bushes?"

"God provides."

"Who is God?"

"God is our Creator. God made this garden, and God made me. God made all the animals, which I named. Then God made you to keep me company." He squeezed her hand and smiled again.

She did not smile. She frowned. She didn't know yet what there could be to do, but surely she couldn't be there just to give Adam someone to show around the garden. Surely if that were all, one of these other animals—the wolf or the horse or the mouse, whatever they were—would be fine.

"Which animal is your favorite?" she asked.

Adam's eyes lit up, and he stopped walking for a moment. "Oh, that'd have to be the dog. Dogs are really sweet." He gave a whistle, and up trotted a four-legged creature, not quite as high as their hips, with hair all over and a smiling, eager-looking face. When the dog saw Adam, he jumped up and placed his forelegs on Adam's shoulders and licked Adam's face.

"Very sweet," she agreed, laughing.

The dog trotted beside them, nudging his head under her hand so that she could stroke it or scratch behind its ears. Adam picked up fallen sticks from the ground and threw them, and the dog would chase them and bring them back, eager for more throwing.

They ducked under a canopy of thick trees. The dog stopped short, staring intently at one of the branches. Then it made a loud, short sound and bounded off after a small creature that scrambled up a tree. Adam told her the name of the small creature was "squirrel."

The river curled into a small pond, barely more than a puddle, and on its banks stood the very largest tree she had seen, with branches that seemed as wide as the sky itself. Large, purple-red fruits hung from its branches, shiny and round and tempting. Enormous deep-green leaves surrounded them, either hiding them or showing them off; she couldn't decide. The scent drifting from the tree was the most enticing in the garden. Sweet but also woodsy, fresh, with a hint of spice that reached her nose only every third breath or so, so she had to go looking for it.

Without conscious thought, her hand stretched out toward the fruit.

"No!" Adam cried, and reached out to grab her wrist.

She turned to him, her hand still hovering. When she saw the fear in Adam's eyes, she dropped her hand.

"This is the fruit," Adam said. "This is the fruit we can't eat!"

"Why not?"

"God says. God says we shouldn't even touch it. Or we'll die."

She didn't understand the word "die," but she could see how frightened Adam was.

She didn't share his fear, though. "Why does it look so delicious?" she asked. "Why would God create such a tempting tree if we couldn't eat from it?" She could hear her own voice; this wasn't just a question of curiosity as the others had been. She felt angry; she felt she was owed an explanation.

"God just did. And God is in charge." A deeply obstinate frown had come over Adam's face, so she decided continuing to argue would be pointless. She'd return to the question of the fruit another day.

"It's getting late. We should find a place to sleep." Adam turned away, passing the tree and heading for the other side of the river.

She took one last glance at the tree, then followed. She saw the sun getting lower and lower in the sky, until it finally disappeared. As it sank, the sky turned all kinds of wonderful colors, from the blue she'd first seen to a sort of orange-pink, then lilac, then settling into a deep, dark blue that was more lovely, to her mind, than the original blue. She and Adam shared their wonderment and delight in the colors. He showed her the medium-sized light, which she named "moon," and all the tiny lights, which he called "stars." They were so spectacular that she wanted to spend all night looking at them, but soon the rhythm of Adam's breathing settled her into sleep.

Only a few hours had passed before she woke again. The sky was still dark blue, so deep now it was nearly black. The moon glowed fiercely, casting their little campground into deep shade and bright light.

Adam slept on.

She breathed in, deep and quiet. A scent wafted to her nostrils—that spice she'd detected, the one near the forbidden tree.

She started to pick her way back toward the tree. She wasn't entirely sure of her way. The garden looked so different at night. She kept pausing to see if she recognized her surroundings.

Finally she came upon the tree. It looked even more magical at night, the moon gilding its leaves and making the translucent fruit seem to glow.

Then she stilled. She heard something in the bushes. A quiet, subtle rustle.

A creature appeared, like one long, curved line, on spindly legs and with tiny little arms. Its long face pointed straight at her, its eyes flickering in her direction. "Hello, Woman," he hissed.

"Are you the Serpent?" she asked.

"I am."

"I'm not supposed to talk to you."

"Says who?"

"Adam. The...you know, the other one like me?"

"What else has Adam told you not to do?" the Serpent asked.

She nodded toward the tree. "He told me not to eat from that fruit of the tree. Or even touch it. Or I'll die." She tried to sound confident, as if she knew what "die" was. Now that she was here in the darkness, next to this sly creature, she recognized in herself the fear she'd seen in Adam's eyes.

But then that scent wafted toward her again. She wondered how bad dying could be, when compared to how good that fruit would taste.

"And who told Adam that?"

"God."

The Serpent hissed, "God doesn't want you to have the knowledge that this tree would give you. God wants to be the only one who knows anything."

She looked from the Serpent to the tree and back again, the questions in her mind too jumbled to come out of her mouth.

The Serpent continued, "This is God's Tree of Knowledge of Good and Evil. If you eat from it, you'll know the things God knows."

"Why wouldn't God want us to know things?"

The Serpent merely shrugged, as best as a creature with no shoulders could shrug.

"Does Adam know that this tree would give us knowledge?"

The Serpent shrugged again. "Your Adam doesn't seem too curious to me."

It was true, he wasn't. But he did seem proud of the knowledge he had. Surely he'd want more?

It was so tempting to just trust the Serpent and take the fruit. "But if I even touch it, I could die," she said, almost to herself.

With the moon glittering off his scales, the Serpent curled its body around the tree and shimmied up to the branch that stretched over her head. "Look at me," the Serpent said from above her. "I'm touching it, and I haven't died. So don't you think you could probably eat from it and not suffer?"

She wanted to resist the urge, she truly did, but the scent was so enticing. Anyway, why exactly couldn't she eat from this tree? This tree would allow her to know things. She and Adam could both know things; she could bring him a piece.

She reached out. Her fingers skimmed the smooth, soft surface of the fruit. Then she grasped the stem. And plucked.

The fruit fell into her hand, glistening like a present intended for her. She barely noticed the Serpent slipping off the tree and disappearing back into the garden. She pressed her lips against the fruit but pulled back at the last minute. She'd wait. She'd eat it with Adam.

She raced back to the campground. The sun was rising, turning the sky orange-pink again, and she could see Adam just stirring as she leapt over a nearby bush to get to him. "Adam, Adam!" she cried, landing in a sort of slide right next to him. "Look at this!"

Adam slowly turned to her and took a deep breath, which brought the scent of the fruit into his nostrils. His eyes widened. "You didn't! We're not supposed to eat from that tree! Or even touch it!"

"I know, I know, but listen, Adam, I haven't eaten from it yet! I wanted to wait and try it with you." He was silent, so she kept talking. "The Serpent, he touched the tree, and nothing happened to him! And it's the Tree of Knowledge of Good and Evil! If we eat from it, we'll know things! We'll know what's right and wrong and the why and how of everything!" She could see he was weakening. She opened her mouth wide and pressed her teeth to the fruit.

"Stop! You'll die!" But Adam couldn't stop looking at the fruit.

"But look, I'm fine. And what is dying, anyway?"

"I don't know." He sounded as if he wanted to learn the answer too.

She sank her teeth into the fruit's flesh. Its taste burst onto her tongue, just like what its scent promised, but even more somehow. Even deeper.

Adam was staring at her, staring at the fruit in her mouth, transfixed. Their eyes met. She held out her hand, held out the fruit to him.

He took a sharp breath in. Then he grasped her wrist, closed his eyes, and bit.

He must have found it as delicious as she had. For a few moments they just sat, chewing together. The juice ran down their throats, and they each quickly went for another bite. They swallowed the whole fruit that way, taking turns, letting the juice run down their fingers.

When the last bite was eaten, they sat for a moment in silence, their sticky fingers entwined. The flavor of the fruit lingered on their tongues, more delicious than any other they'd tasted. They laughed together, shocked by their daring, bonded in their mutual rebellion. For the first time, she felt that she was not created for Adam, but that they were created for each other.

A strong wind blew. The air changed. That magical scent seemed to drift away, leaving in its place something bracing and sharp. They looked at each other, suddenly horrified. They scooted apart and crouched in the bushes, far away from each other.

"Adam! You're naked!"

"So are you!"

"Well, how do we..." Then they both fell silent. They heard a rustle through the bushes. It wasn't the Serpent. It wasn't a horse or a squirrel or a dog either. She looked at Adam.

Adam's eyes went wide. "It's God."

She had never met God before. She trembled a bit. Then she felt a sort of warmth, a strength, and a comfort surrounding her.

"Where are you?" A deep voice seemed to come from all around them.

Adam spoke first. "We're here, God. In the bushes."

She sensed that the presence was closer.

"Why do you hide from me, Adam?" the voice intoned.

"Because I'm naked."

There was a stillness, a silence. Then, "How did you know you were naked? Did you eat from the tree I told you not to eat from?"

Adam glared at her from behind his bush, looking panicked. She could only look back at him.

"The woman, the woman you put in the garden with me, she gave me the fruit."

Oh, nice, Adam. Way to make this all my fault. Or God's fault.

"Is that true, Woman?"

Should she do the same as Adam? "Yes. Your creature, the Serpent, he showed me that the fruit was good, so I ate it."

"The Serpent?" The air rippled heat. God was angry. "I'll deal with him later."

Then the presence cooled again, and the voice became comforting. "Woman, Adam, why did you do this? Tell me."

She decided she could speak first this time. "I wanted to know things, God. I wanted to know why the sun set and how to make more fruit appear on the bushes and why you created me and Adam and what we should be doing here. The Serpent told me that if I ate the fruit, I'd know everything."

"And do you?"

She thought for a moment. "No. But I know more. And I think I can learn and discover."

God sighed deeply. It was as if all the air in the garden contracted, and then released. "Well, you're going to have to learn and discover now, aren't you? You can't stay in this lovely garden now that you've eaten the fruit of knowledge."

Was there someplace else, other than this garden?

She glanced at Adam, questions in her eyes. Adam shrugged, his brow furrowed. He didn't know, either.

But God could hear her unspoken thoughts. "Oh, yes, there's a world beyond this garden. In this garden, I provided you with everything you needed. You were warm and comfortable, safe and well fed, and you didn't have to worry about any of it. But out there? Out there, you'll have to grow your own food, with sweat and effort. You'll have to create a shelter, and you'll have to protect yourselves from wild animals. You'll have to bear children, who will one day leave you, too, no matter how beautiful a garden you build for them. And yes, you will grow old and eventually die. You have no idea how much there will be to learn and discover."

Adam looked more frightened with every word that God spoke. But she couldn't help a growing feeling of excitement welling up in her belly. So much to learn and discover? God seemed to think it was a threat, but it sounded thrilling to her.

And yes, a little scary.

But she had already learned something, she thought. She no longer felt the need to ask what dying was. She couldn't say she knew, exactly, but she sensed what it was now. An ending of some kind. And she and Adam could make their own decisions. Build their own gardens. Make more people. Learn about the stars and the sun.

Adam kept his head bent. "I'm sorry, God," he said, and so she adopted a similar posture and mumbled something about "sorry," too. She was, a little. God sounded sad as well as angry, and she hadn't wanted to make God sad.

"You'd best be on your way, then," God said. "I have to go talk to the Serpent."

Adam cleared his throat. "Um...God? We're still naked."

God had sounded so upset about them leaving the garden; she assumed God would just tell them that getting un-naked was their own problem. But God fashioned clothing for them from the leaves of the Tree of Knowledge of Good and Evil. Then God led them to the gates of the garden wall and bid them goodbye.

"You can never return to the Garden of Eden," God said, "but I'm always here if you need Me. Just call out to Me, and I will send you help. And tell your children to do the same, and tell them to tell their children, that I will be a Help for them forever."

She and Adam were too choked up to say anything, but they nodded and waved. Out here, outside the walls, God's presence seemed more distant, and the land less giving. But they would learn—together.

She turned to Adam. "I forgot to ask God. I don't have a name."

Adam grinned at her. "Oh, I had an idea for that. I thought, since you will be the mother of all life that you should be called Eve. Eve means 'life.'"

Eve grinned. She could feel already that the name was right. And they set off together into the world, to learn things and make things all on their own.

CHAPTER TWO

Noah's Hope

Had it really rained for forty days and forty nights? That's what they'd say later, but Noah didn't really know if that was true. How could you tell day from night when the whole world turned black, when all that surrounded you was water, when every living thing left in the whole world was aboard the boat that God told you to build?

Except for fish. Noah had seen fish in the waters below. Perhaps they thought they were now God's chosen creatures—the whole world remade for them.

Then the rain simply stopped. One minute, it was a downpour, it was sheets of driving water; it was howling wind and lashing waves and an endless rushing, pounding noise that could make you think you had ceased to exist. You were the rain now, and the rain was you.

And then, nothing. In the blink of an eye, sunshine and calm waters and quiet. You could think again. You could hear individual animals, groaning and growling and yelping. They had been silent since the rain started. At least Noah thought they had been silent. Maybe he simply couldn't hear them over the rain.

Noah stood. It took a while. He was old and, after being on the boat so long, stiff. He groaned. Then he groaned louder, the very sound of his voice like a reassurance that he existed. He *wasn't* rain, after all. He was Noah.

He peered out the window. Bright, cheery sunshine, the kind that should make his heart glad. But it was shining on nothing but water, as far as the eye could see. No shining silver-green leaf danced before his eye. No mountain grew tall and proud with its crowning halo. No red rooftop was warmed by the sun's rays. The endless water left him reeling, the pit of his stomach swirling as if the boat were still being tossed about on the storm-raging waves. For a moment, his vision went as black as if the sun were still hidden from him.

And then, a knock. A quiet knock on his door, as if from a very small hand. He had come on this ark with his three sons and their three wives, and two of those wives had been escorting children, including his first grandchild, Japheth's oldest, Eli. Eli's warm brown eyes and kind voice lighted Noah's whole heart.

Eli was old enough that he had been around to help Noah at the last stages of building the ark, an arduous process that had taken years and years and years. Truthfully, Noah had stretched it out as long as he could. He kept hoping that his neighbors would take the time he was giving them to listen to the voice of God, to turn away from their evil ways, to make amends and atone.

"It is futile," God told Noah. "They have nothing but wickedness in their hearts. They lie and steal, they abuse their animals and their neighbors, they neglect their children. They feel no remorse when another is hurt by their actions."

But Noah insisted on giving them every chance. He even said he would grow fresh trees to make the ark, so that his neighbors would have the time it would take to grow the trees, to repent and make amends. So God sighed and said that Noah's good heart was why God considered him the only righteous man, and God let Noah have his way. How important was the length of time it took to grow a tree, after all, to the Eternal?

Noah planted the trees. Then he waited for them to grow, and grow, and grow some more. They had to be big trees, didn't they, to build such an ark as God wanted? Three hundred cubits long, God had said, and fifty cubits wide, and thirty cubits high. That was a lot of cubits. So it took many years to grow the cedars so big.

Then Noah began to build the ark. He set himself up not far from the village center, so that all of his neighbors could see him and ask what he was doing. It was a curious thing to be building a boat so far from the sea, so many of them did stop and ask.

Though their questions carried more jeering than sincerity, Noah always told them the truth. "As God has told you, God is soon sending a flood, to sweep the earth of wickedness. God has ordered me to build an ark to keep my family safe and to keep two of each animal safe. But if you atone and make amends for your wickedness, God will not send a flood." Then he would invite them to pray with him. They never did.

As his neighbors continued to snicker at him behind their hands, Noah continued to build. Sometimes he'd come to the site of the boat in the morning and find that his tools had been stolen. It didn't bother him, at least not much. He even began leaving them out overnight on purpose, because if someone stole them, he'd have to get new tools, which would take extra time, which would give his neighbors time for *t'shuvah*, for seeking forgiveness for their wicked ways and for turning toward righteousness. Still, it wasn't lost on him that if they were stealing his tools, they were no closer to atonement than they had ever been.

It also didn't bother him when they started throwing rotten food at him and at the boat when he was working. When a boat was being made to withstand a world-destroying flood, what did a bit of rotten fig on the hull matter?

One morning, Noah arrived at the boat site to find something worse than rotten figs. He found the hull smashed to pieces, shards and splinters scattered angrily about the ground. It was violent and nasty in a way that figs just weren't. Noah felt an anger rise in his belly—a rage, a pillar of fire. He wanted to unleash it on his neighbors, howl and fury until they were all blown away. And what was Noah's anger, compared to the anger of God, who had created humanity with hope and love, only to have them choose wickedness?

But Noah was a kind man, a patient man, a righteous man. Noah took a long, deep breath. And then another, and another, and another, until the fires of rage were banked. He reminded himself that having to repair the hull would only further delay the flood. So Noah kept steadily on. He would not falter. He would simply trust God and hope that his neighbors would see the errors of their ways before it was too late.

And then Eli came along—his first son's first son, such a blessing. A promise from God, Noah felt, that there would be a future ahead for this boy. When Eli was old enough, he would toddle along to Noah's work site and watch him. He would grab tools and Noah would grab them back. They were dangerous in a baby's hands, of course, but also the longer Noah played vigorous games of "Mine!" the longer the building of the boat would take.

When Eli was old enough to imitate Noah's actions, to run his hand along a plank as Noah sanded or to wield a brush to paint the boards with the sap that would keep them watertight, Noah allowed him to help. Certainly Eli helping took longer than Eli not helping. But taking longer was the goal. And Noah enjoyed Eli's sweet face, with the endless questions issuing from Eli's mouth.

"Why do the cedars smell so good?" Eli asked him.

"To make our work more pleasant," Noah answered.

"How will we stop the lions from eating the lambs on the ark?"

"God has commanded that they be kept on separate decks, so that the animals will not eat or hurt each other."

"Can we get some cake when we are done?"

"Of course."

"What will we eat on the ark?"

Oh dear. Not cake, that was a certainty. "God will provide."

As the ark was coming to completion, Noah's stomach roiled with conflicting feelings. On the one hand, he was angry at his neighbors, for their violent and destructive behavior, their carelessness, their utter failure to do anything kind or helpful. On the other hand, he felt sorry for them. Soon they would simply be gone—wiped from the face of the earth. No one would remember them. No children would carry them in their hearts, tell the next generation about them, think of them fondly.

Sometimes Noah even felt angry at God, for the flood God would soon bring. But then a large stone would whiz past Noah's head from the thicket of trees that Noah himself had planted, where a neighbor was hiding, jeering, looking for more rocks to throw, and Noah's anger would transfer back to his neighbors again.

Sometimes Noah thought he was doing the wrong thing—building this ark, getting on it, saving himself when he knew all these people would die.

But then Eli would come along and take his hand, asking for cake, and Noah would feel as though the light of God itself had entered his belly. For him, then. For this child, he could build this ark, he could gather animals, he could secure a future. Maybe the people would hear the voice of God and turn away from their wicked ways, and then Eli could grow up among the righteous. And if they wouldn't, then Noah would whisk Eli away from them, let him start a new world, a world full of wondering eyes and diligent hands and kind hearts.

As God had warned Noah, the people never did turn away from their wickedness. Even when the ark was complete, they watched Noah load the animals, laughing still, though more cruelly, more angrily. Noah brought his family onto the ark and then lingered at the doorway, pulling up the gangway slowly, giving them all a last chance. They only sneered. So Noah boarded up the door.

The moment the last nail had been hammered in place, the rain came. It started as suddenly as it would stop, forty days later. The heavens opened up, and the water crashed down on the people who were standing on what was rapidly becoming the banks of a sea. Then the people turned their furious eyes to the boat and rushed at it. Noah thought for a moment that they were trying to get in. But they weren't. They were only trying to tip the boat over. If they were going to be destroyed, they wanted everything destroyed. Wicked, through and through.

And now, now that the deluge was over, Eli was here yet again, knocking at his door. "Grandpa?" he said.

Noah rushed—as much as his old bones could rush—to the door. "I'm here, Eli. I'm here. Are you okay?"

Eli let out a shaky sigh and nodded his unsteady head. "It's over," he said.

Noah looked out the window. "So it is."

"Can we go up on the deck now?"

So Noah took his grandson's hand in his—such a small, soft hand in Noah's worn one—and they went up to the deck together. Soon the rest of the family joined them. They stood together for several minutes, basking in the sun.

Then an animal yowled, and they all went down to see which one and what needed to be done about it.

They would not see land for several months, but they kept busy. The lions, as it happened, did not try to eat the lambs. Every animal seemed content to eat the hay that Noah had stored before the rain. Noah assumed that God was keeping the peace from the heavens, but there was still quite a lot to do. The ark had to be kept sealed with the mixture of charcoal and sap that Noah had brought aboard. The animals had to be kept clean and well-groomed. Their pens also had to be kept clean, which was the most disagreeable chore.

They sent out a raven, but the raven just flew and flew, having found no tree on which to perch. They sent out a dove, but it came back. Another brought back a branch from an olive tree. The branch became a centerpiece on the ark, a sign of hope. A tree was sighted at last, its trunk submerged but the tips of its branches reaching up to the sun.

The next dove didn't come back at all. It had found a place to perch. Noah and Eli watched the skies for days, smiling at each other when they remained empty.

And they stood together the day the boat bumped into land and a rainbow stretched across the sky. "This rainbow is the symbol of God's promise," Noah told Eli. "God is promising never to flood the world again. God is promising us a future." But Noah already had all the promise he needed as he held Eli's hand in his.

CHAPTER THREE

Go Forth and Smash the Idols!

WHEN ABRAM MET HIS WIFE, SARAI, HE THOUGHT ALL HIS prayers were answered. Sarai was unlike anyone Abram had met before. She was strong and brave, intelligent and kind. Sarai thought Abram was special too. He was patient and clever. He wasn't scared of meeting new people or exploring new places. He wasn't afraid to think for himself or to share what he was thinking. More importantly, Abram and Sarai shared a vision for their life together. They wanted to go on adventures, to help people, and to have a big family.

Abram wanted his home to be just as hectic and noisy as his own had been, with his two brothers. Sarai was an only child, which she had found too quiet and sometimes lonely.

"I hope we have a dozen sons just like you," Sarai said to Abram.

And Abram replied, "I hope we have a dozen daughters just like you." They laughed for a long time; a dozen children sounded ridiculous.

Abram and Sarai wanted to start their family right away, but it seemed to be taking longer than they had hoped.

"Maybe this means we should go on our adventures first," said Sarai, and Abram agreed.

Abram's father, Terach, was a sculptor. He made statues of all the gods that people prayed to in their hometown of Ur. Terach invited his sons' families to travel with him to Haran, stopping to sell god-statues along the way.

People would buy the god-statues, set them up in their homes, and pray to them for blessings: good health, good fortune, a plentiful harvest, or healthy children. Sometimes people left gifts at the god-statues' feet: meat, vegetables, handfuls of grain, or even a jug of wine, in case the god-statue got hungry or thirsty.

Abram and Sarai loved traveling with their big family—by then they had lots of nieces and nephews—and meeting the people who bought god-statues from Terach. But soon they noticed that although most people prayed to the god-statues and brought them gifts, the god-statues didn't seem to answer. Many people they met had bad harvests and were poor and hungry. Some had children who were sick, and others, like Abram and Sarai, worried that they might not be able to have children at all.

When customers complained to Terach that the god-statues weren't working, Terach told them, "You must pray harder and bring more gifts." Or he might pick up a different god-statue: "Try this one."

One day Abram said to Sarai, "There has to be another way to help people, when the god-statues aren't able to." And Sarai agreed. They set up a tent next to Terach's shop, where they offered food and drink to people who were hungry or thirsty, herbs and ointments for people who were sick or hurt, or simply a place to sit and rest and share their troubles.

When their guests reached for a few coins to thank Sarai and Abram for their hospitality, Abram would wave them away. "No charge," he said. "Just give thanks to God for your blessings."

Some guests asked, "Which god?"

"Just God," Abram replied. "The One who created the world and all its blessings."

"And where is this God?" the guests would ask.

"Everywhere," Abram would say. "But this God can't be seen."

The guests shrugged and looked at him sideways. They didn't understand. Sometimes, even after Abram told them about the One God, they still went to Terach's shop to choose a god-statue. Abram and Sarai's generosity was good for Terach's business.

One afternoon Abram stood at the opening of the tent, watching people go in and out of his father's shop. "I know it sounds crazy," he said to Sarai, "but I believe there is only one God, who created the world, and hears our prayers, and grants us blessings."

Sarai stood beside him. "I don't think that's crazy."

But Abram wasn't finished. "And I don't think God eats food or drinks wine. Or that we can hold God in our hands like a statue. What if God is much bigger than that?"

At these words, Sarai began to cry. She reached into her satchel and pulled out a small statue of a woman with wide hips and a round belly—a goddess-statue for fertility. "I've been praying to her every night for us to have a child," Sarai said through her tears. "I give her food and wine and bow before her. I pray with all my heart, and still nothing." Angrily she tossed the goddess-statue at Abram, and he caught it. He put one arm around Sarai, hugging her, trying to comfort her, and staring at the statue as she cried on his shoulder.

Suddenly Abram became enraged. He was mad at the god-statues for being useless. He was mad at his father for selling them and at his customers for buying them. He was mad at himself for letting himself be duped. He was even mad at God, the real God, for not answering his prayers. He lifted the statue high above his head, then threw it at the ground as hard as he could. It shattered into a thousand pieces. Startled, Sarai looked up at him.

"That...felt...incredible!" Abram was breathless with relief.

Sarai sniffled and stood up. "Maybe I could try it too?"

The sun was setting, and Terach had gone back to his tent for supper. Abram and Sarai snuck into the shop, where they found a whole rack of round goddess-statues. Sarai lifted one of them gingerly with both hands. With a teary smile, she smashed it against the hard ground. The crash was so satisfying that she picked up another, and another, until there were none left on the shelf.

Then Abram grabbed one of the harvest gods, which had left so many people hungry even after they prayed for food, a god that demanded offerings of grain even when people barely had enough for themselves. "You're a phony and a fake," he shouted as he hurled it to the ground. Soon they were smashing every god-statue in the store.

They were about to knock down the biggest god-statue when Abram stopped and looked around in horror at the mess they had made. It felt great while they were doing it, and Abram was sure they had done the right thing. But he doubted that his father would agree. "What are we going to do?" he cried. "What will we tell my father?"

"Wait!" cried Sarai. "I have an idea." She took a big stick and threaded it through the statue's hands. Then she grabbed Abram, and they hurried back to their tent.

In the morning, Terach's furious cries echoed throughout the camp. Abram, his brothers, and their wives rushed in to see what had happened.

"Who did this?" Terach fumed. "Who destroyed my god-statues?"

Abram stepped forward and pointed at the remaining god-statue, just as he and Sarai had discussed. "Don't you see?" he said cautiously. "The gods got into a fight over who was the most powerful, and this god won!" Abram knew that he should have felt guilty about lying to his father, but weren't the god-statues an even bigger lie?

Terach was not convinced. "That's ridiculous!" he yelled. "They're statues! They can't talk. They certainly can't fight. They can't do anything!"

Now it was Sarai's turn to step forward. "If that's true," she said, her voice trembling, "why do we pray to them for blessings?"

Terach fell silent, his face red with rage. Sarai had been right: even if he suspected that one of his children had broken the god-statues, he'd never admit it.

"Clean up this mess!" he grumbled, stomping out of the shop. Abram's brothers and their wives left Abram and Sarai alone to pick up the pieces. Only his nephew, Lot, stayed to help. "I never thought these statues could do anything, either," he whispered, sweeping up the shards with a broom.

It was evening when the three of them left the shop. The setting sun turned the distant mountains a fiery pink. "It's so beautiful," Sarai sighed.

And Abram agreed. "There must be one God who created all of this," he said. "It's too magnificent to come from a statue. Or even a bunch of statues. That's who deserves our thanks. That's who we should ask for blessings."

Then Abram heard a voice: "Go forth from your homeland, from the place you were born, and from your father's house, to the land that I will show you."

The voice sounded like nothing Abram had ever heard before. It sounded like the crash of thunder, and like gentle ocean waves, and like the beating of Sarai's heart. He turned to Sarai and Lot. "Did you hear that?"

Sarai and Lot stood, nearly frozen behind Abram, unable to speak. Even if they hadn't heard the voice, something powerful was happening to them too. Abram knew right away that this voice belonged to God. Not to a clay statue, not to a god of harvests or healing or fertility, but to the one true God of everything.

For years, the people around Abram and Sarai had been asking the god-statues to give them blessings. But the god-statues never talked back. This time God spoke directly to him, asking him to do something difficult. Abram tried to steady himself as his whole body shook. He was terrified.

"If I go with You, if Sarai and I agree to follow You," Abram asked, "will you give us Your blessing?"

"I will make you a great nation," God promised. "I will make your name great. And you shall *be* a blessing."

"What does that mean?" Sarai asked. "What does it mean to be a blessing?"

God's voice was gentle. "It means that I have chosen you both to walk on a sacred path with Me, so that together we can make the world a better place. It means you will go on many adventures and know both great joy and unimaginable challenges. It means that there will be new rules to follow and old traditions to break. It means that you will always be a little different from the people around you, so you might be lonely much of the time. It means that sometimes what I ask you to do will be difficult, because it's not what everyone else is doing. Sometimes people will want to fight you when you stand up for what is right. You will have to learn when to fight back, when to walk away, and when to make peace, even when you don't agree. It means that you will have to go far away from the people you love, so that you can help people in every corner of the earth. It means I may not always give you everything you ask for. But I will give you a chance to make a difference. I will give you a chance to heal this broken world."

Abram thought that this was better than any of the blessings he and Sarai had asked for. The world needed so much help and healing, and the idea of being part of that made him feel less helpless, less angry, and less alone. The god-statues couldn't help people. But he and Sarai could.

Sarai took his hand, and he knew that she agreed. Someday they would know the blessing of having a child. But for now, they held hands and took that first step forward, to follow God and change the world.

CHAPTER FOUR

Rebecca Goes Forth

THE DAY WAS HOT EVEN BEFORE THE SUN HAD CLEARED THE line of mountains in the distance. The faint taste of sand was at the back of Rebecca's throat; it was the driest of the dry season. Still, Rebecca went about her tasks with her usual diligence. She fed the goats their breakfast and refilled their trough. They bleated happily at her. All of them looked healthy and well rested, which made her smile. Sometimes she liked to imagine that the goats were children, and she was the matriarch of a large, prosperous clan, seeing to her family's needs and wishes, as well as the needs and wishes of the whole community, giving good cheer and receiving nothing but gratitude in return. The goats, at least, made this particular flight of fancy easy.

Then she went into her father's room. Her father had been more or less bedridden these past few years. He'd suffered a foot injury and then a nasty ailment in his lungs and throat, and he'd never fully recovered from either.

He had once been so hale and hearty, quick with a joke, wrestling with even the largest of their herd, putting his considerable strength into the same tasks even the lowliest servants did, in order to make work as light as possible for everyone. Now he could hardly shuffle out of bed most days. It made Rebecca want to cry, but she didn't want him to see her upset, so she brought a smile into the room with her, along with clean water.

Her mother was also already up, mending tent cloth in light that was not nearly adequate. Rebecca tutted and opened the tent flap farther to let in the weak morning sun, but she knew she could not stop her mother from doing work she ought to be passing off to a servant by now. Rebecca also knew she would probably be the same when she was an old lady, insisting on seeing to her tasks even when it would be better for everyone if someone else took over.

Rebecca set herself to grinding the berries she and her mother had dried, making a paste that could be used to dye cloth. As she worked, she imagined herself combining this paste with other colors and creating cloaks of various colors for all the children of her clan. Well, maybe that would be too much. Maybe a little doll each. Or maybe she'd use these berries and a goodly amount of sumac and knead them into bread. She'd be known from town to town for the deliciousness of her bread; strangers would come in from their travels having the scent already in their nostrils. And she'd be able to serve them on fine clay platters with serving spoons of cedar, loaded with figs and barley, and perhaps extra little dyed dolls for their children.

Her vision of herself as a bountiful and beneficent hostess was interrupted, as it often was, by her brother Laban. He bounced into the kitchen with a cheerful smile. That raised Rebecca's hackles immediately. A cheerful Laban usually meant trouble for Rebecca. Then again, so did a grumpy Laban. Or a sad Laban. Or an enraged Laban. Really, the only Laban that didn't trouble Rebecca was a sleeping Laban.

Still, Rebecca would try. She always did. She used to think that if she was just kind enough to her brother, that if she met him with gentleness, with smiles, with good humor, then he would be inspired to behave better. She didn't really believe that anymore. When had she given up? Was it when he slid into their father's place at the dinner table, just after their father had injured his foot? Or when he tripped her as she struggled under the weight of water jugs that were bigger than she was? Or was it when he'd kicked the smallest of the newborn goats, straight into a prickly hedge, and then laughed?

That was probably it. The hedge. The poor goat had a bloodied eye and never walked without a limp after that.

Still, even if she had lost hope of him ever improving, it didn't mean she should respond in kind. So she was determined to greet him each morning, at least, with polite calm.

"Good morning, Laban," she said with a smile that was only a little stiff. "How did you sleep?"

"Morning, Becs!" Ugh, she hated when he called her Becs. And he followed it with a big slap on her back, right between the shoulder blades, nearly knocking her down.

"Laban!" she shrieked. All right, so her resolve to be nice to him every day rarely lasted past their first interaction.

"Don't yell at your brother," their mother said mildly, bustling over to the kitchen. She gave her son a hug and a kiss. "You want breakfast, my darling boy?"

"Mama, you should sit," Rebecca said. "I'll get breakfast ready." She ignored that angry twinge that always flared when her mother treated Laban as if he were the morning sun and the evening stars. It was just a twinge now; she used to rail at her mother. But her mother would cluck at Rebecca and tell her how hard the only son had it, how much responsibility he had on his shoulders. Then, once their father was injured, their mother had clucked over Laban as if Laban were the patient.

Rebecca set the pot boiling and added the barley. She had brought plentiful water up from the well yesterday—four whole jugs of it, so she wouldn't have to go for another few days. The well was a good twenty-minute walk from the house. You had to walk down the hill, fill your jug, bring it to the top, repeat. Full, the jugs weighed nearly as much as Rebecca herself. Then you had to lug them home. Her shoulders were still sore today.

Laban leaned over her shoulder—too close. When they were younger, Rebecca would have elbowed him in the ribs for standing this close, especially because she knew he was only doing it to annoy her. But he'd gotten too big, and Rebecca was trying to turn herself into the kind of woman who could be that generous matriarch she imagined. Generous matriarchs didn't elbow their brothers in the ribs. "Did you put enough salt in?"

He was only needling her. She should remain calm. "I'm sure I did, dear brother," she said through clenched teeth. "If you're unsure, you can take over the making of the breakfast." She meant to make it sound like a sweet, genuine offer, but it most certainly didn't.

"Mom!" he yelled directly into her ear, a little too loud, on purpose.

"Mom, Rebecca's messing up the barley! I don't think she knows how to make it as well as you do!"

Sure enough, their mother bustled over. "I'll fix it for you, honey," she said, patting Laban's cheek.

"Mom, you should really sit. I can do this," Rebecca said, but her mother waved her off.

"It's my pleasure to make a delicious meal for my darling child—children." She clearly thought she covered her mistake, but Rebecca heard it. So did Laban. He smirked at Rebecca.

Rebecca pretended not to notice and returned to her berries. They were almost ready to steep in vinegar. But Laban, not one to rest when there was more he could do to make Rebecca's life difficult, stalked over to the four nearly full jugs of water. "Hey, this is great, Becs! I was hoping to bathe today!"

And then Laban took his entire arm—his dirty, sandy arm with its grimy, smelly hand—and stuck it directly into the fresh jug of water.

Don't react, don't react, don't react. But she was on the verge; she could feel it.

Then he stuck his equally disgusting foot in a *second* jug and splashed her with the water!

"It's refreshing, Becs, isn't it?" And he laughed, like a delighted four-year-old, instead of the obstreperous full-grown man he was.

"I just brought that water up yesterday," she said under her breath, though why she bothered, she couldn't imagine.

"Now, children," their mother said with a fond chuckle, as if she too thought they were a pair of playful babies.

"He's not a child, Mother," Rebecca snapped. She felt guilty immediately; her ire should be directed at Laban, not their mother. But words were pouring out anyway. "He's old enough to be married, old enough to have a wife and children to torture instead of me!" Though she pitied the children who would one day call Laban "Father."

"Rebecca! Lower your voice; your father is sleeping!"

Her father, in his decline, couldn't really hear her anyway, but Rebecca took a deep breath and gathered herself together—that is, until Laban, either in his clumsiness or on purpose, waved a hand wildly and knocked the crushed berries into the third jug.

Whether it had been on purpose or not, Laban was in no way sorry. "Oh, no! Guess you'll have to go back to the well today!" And he grinned.

Rebecca let out a loud shriek, right in her brother's face, and felt a small degree of childish glee even as her mother scolded her. Then she fetched some empty jugs from the side of the house and marched herself down to the well.

The walk to the well calmed her a bit, especially as she allowed her mind to wander to her fantasy life, in which she was the kind and generous head of a large and expansive family. What sort of man would be standing by her side? He'd have to be kind and generous too, of course. Perhaps with an easy humor, like her father? Oh, but she could also see herself falling in love with someone with a hint of sadness to him, someone who needed her to brighten his spirits and comfort his sorrows. She sighed. She could be such a good wife, and she was of an age to be married too. But they lived in such a remote place; where would she even find a husband?

And then, bizarrely, she saw a strange man sitting on the parapet near the well, two camels nearby. As she approached, she dismissed him as the possible husband made manifest by her imagination. He was far too old, nearly of an age with her father. And he wore a band around his upper arm that Rebecca had been told the servants and slaves of rich men sometimes wore. Still, he was a new person, which was interesting, at the very least. And of course, he and his camels must be thirsty. An opportunity, then, for Rebecca to be the gracious hostess she wanted to be.

She ignored the groaning in her shoulders and pressed forward.

"Good day, *adon*," Rebecca said, using a polite form of address. She didn't know if calling a servant "lord" was exactly proper, but she thought it would be better to be too respectful than too diminishing. "Have you traveled far?"

The man looked up, somewhat startled. Maybe he'd started to doze, sitting there. "Oh. Yes. Yes, miss. From Canaan."

Rebecca murmured in recognition. She thought her father had an uncle living there, but she couldn't remember for sure. "Can I get you some water?"

He nodded gratefully, so she went down to the bottom of the hill, filled the first jug, and hauled it up the hill. He had a goblet with him, made of fine, smooth cedar wood, and he drank thirstily, murmuring his thanks between every gulp—just the way she had always imagined a gracious hostess would be treated. She felt a thrill even as she recognized her childishness.

While the man drank, Rebecca filled the second jug and hauled it up, placing it between his camels. They also somehow managed to convey gratitude from beneath their ridiculous eyelashes, and Rebecca chuckled a little. She scratched them behind the ears and muttered encouraging words to them.

When the man finished drinking, she knelt to use the rest of the water to wash his feet. It was more a gesture of hospitality than a purposeful cleaning, as he would still have to walk on from here to his destination, but it was what a good hostess did, and she was determined that she not fail in any of the kind gestures now that she had an opportunity to practice them.

"May I ask the name of the woman whose generosity I am experiencing?"

"Rebecca, daughter of Bethuel, son of Milcah and Nahor."

"I see. You are kind indeed, Rebecca."

"It is nothing," she said modestly.

The camels finished their water and seemed to be licking the very splinters off the jug, so Rebecca went down and hauled another serving up for them. Then she took the now-empty vat she'd used for the man's feet and filled it for her family, though she did check to see if the man wanted more water first.

"I should introduce myself," he said. "I am Eliezer, servant of your great-uncle Abraham, son of Terach."

"Oh! I thought my great-uncle was Abram?"

"Yes. That was his name. But Adonai, our God, gave him a new name, because Abraham is to be Adonai's prophet."

Rebecca wrinkled her brow. She had not heard of this "Adonai" before, though she did hear that her uncle Abram—Abraham—had smashed her grandfather's idols before he left Haran. Maybe this Adonai was the reason. She thought about the house idols that her brother Laban held so dear. Perhaps her uncle had the right idea about them. Perhaps this Adonai was indeed a better choice.

"I have come here seeking a wife for Abraham's son, Isaac." The servant raised his eyes at Rebecca. "And he encouraged me to look among Nahor's descendants."

"Oh!" Rebecca was dumbfounded for a moment, coming to the understanding that this man, this servant of her uncle's, meant her—meant that *she* could be a bride to this Isaac.

She set her jugs down. Her mind now raced. So many questions were circling her thoughts that she couldn't pick one to focus on. How old was Isaac? Did he want a wife? Was he... she thought of her vision of her future, of being a matriarch, a blessing to her community. Was he a man who was interested in such a life? How did he treat the people around him?

Had he ever kicked a goat?

"I had added a wish when I prayed to Adonai to help me in a quest for young Isaac's wife," the man continued, taking her hands in his. Rebecca was startled for a moment, but she listened. "I prayed for a wife for him who was kind, and generous, and strong. I thought to myself, if she offers me a drink and also offers drinks to my camels, I will know she is the one Adonai has chosen for Isaac. And you have shown yourself to be these things. Adonai has truly blessed my quest."

Rebecca blushed furiously, both mightily pleased and equally embarrassed to have her actions praised so thoroughly.

"May I come with you to your parents' home and ask them if I might take you to my master's son?"

"Of course," she said, almost automatically. She was distracted for a moment by the thought that if her brother hadn't deliberately antagonized her that morning, she might not have come to the well today. She might not have met this man.

She refused to feel any gratitude toward Laban though. Perhaps she should feel gratitude to this Adonai instead, if indeed Eliezer's prayers were what drew Rebecca to the well.

"But first," the servant said, and he reached into one of the camel's saddlebags, pulling out two bangles. He slipped one over each of Rebecca's wrists. "A gift from my master. I come with much in the way of bride price, if that will sway your family to part with you." Eliezer gestured to his camels, which were indeed laden with fine-looking blankets and decorative bags of richly embroidered leather. She looked down at the beautifully wrought gold and silver bracelets on her wrists. Yes, this sort of bride price might sway even Laban to let her go.

She realized she was already assuming she would go. She was even excited about going—about the chance to go to a future that wasn't here, in this lonely little encampment, with her hideous brother, and with limited opportunities to practice her natural instincts for caretaking.

Would going with Eliezer give her the opportunities she craved? "What sort of man is Isaac?" she asked, as Eliezer took pace beside her, holding one of her jugs.

"He is young, not much older than you," Eliezer began. "I have known him since he was born. He was a lively child. Playful and mischievous. But he is sad now. I am hoping that bringing him a wife will cheer him up."

Rebecca felt her heart soften. "Why is he sad?"

"His mother has passed, only just. And he and his father... well... let us simply say they do not speak now."

"Why not?"

Eliezer hesitated, and Rebecca nudged him with her elbow. "Come, it is a long walk to my father's tent. You might as well tell me."

"There was a miscommunication," Eliezer said. "My lord Abraham believed that Adonai wanted him to take Isaac up a mountain and sacrifice him."

"What?!"

"Yes. And, well, the mistake was corrected, of course, but not before Abraham had tied Isaac to an altar and raised a knife to him."

Oh dear. Rebecca's heart melted further. What a horror for a young person to endure. And then she made another connection. "Does Isaac know his father has sent you to seek a wife for him?"

Eliezer shrugged. "He will be glad to have one."

"Eliezer! He doesn't know?! What are you going to do, just drop me off in front of his tent?"

Eliezer laughed, and it was a rich, warm laugh. "He will be happy, I assure you. He loves and trusts me, and he trusts Adonai. After all, Adonai stopped Abraham's hand."

Well, that was a wrinkle Rebecca was not expecting. Could she just show up and offer herself as wife to a person who didn't even know he was seeking one?

Still... she could cheer him up. She could make him smile after his loss. That was tempting.

Rebecca hitched the stranger's camels to the posts outside their tent and lifted the tent flap. Laban was comfortably ensconced in their father's best chair, and he glared as they came in.

"Who is this, and what is he doing here?" Laban demanded.

"Eliezer, my brother Laban," Rebecca said swiftly. "Let me go get Father."

She guided her father in a few moments later. He was confused but seemed content nonetheless. He patted her hand and murmured things that sounded like the pet names he had had for her as a child.

Laban didn't move even when he saw his father, so Rebecca said, "Laban, Father needs the chair," with as little emotion as she could. Laban did stand then, keeping his eye on Eliezer the whole time.

Rebecca introduced Eliezer to her curious mother and her decidedly unconcerned father. Then Eliezer explained his purpose. Rebecca showed her bangles, which made Laban's eyes go wide.

Then Laban stiffened. In the battle between wanting more riches and wanting to ruin his sister's happiness, the latter force was winning. "You can't go with him," he said. "It's ludicrous. How do we even know he is who he says he is?"

Their father spoke, suddenly, almost lucidly. "I remember you," he said. "You were so small the last time I saw you."

Eliezer grinned. "Yes, *adon*. I got bigger. You, on the other hand, seem to have gotten smaller." There was a teasing light in his eyes, and Rebecca's father laughed. It was the most joy she'd seen on his face in a long time.

Laban continued huffing. "What about us? Rebecca takes care of us; who's going to do it when she's not here?"

"I thought I wasn't good enough to make your barley," Rebecca retorted. Then she colored. Would Eliezer think her less kind than he had before?

But his eyes were twinkling, and he was nodding approvingly.

"Mother!" Laban turned to their mother. "Tell her she can't go!"

Perhaps for the first time, their mother did not take Laban's side in an argument. "Laban, she has to get married sometime. And you know *I* can take care of you."

"Father? You don't want her to leave, do you? She cleans your feet, she washes your linens, she makes most meals."

But her father shook his head and patted Rebecca on the arm. "Whatever you want, dear heart," he said. Then he promptly fell asleep on the chair.

Laban stuck his chest out, strutting. "Well, I am the man of the house now, and it's my decision. And I decide—"

But Rebecca shot her hand out toward him. A surge of triumph roared through her. "No, Laban. It's my decision. And I have decided. *Eileich.*" *I will go.* She liked the short efficiency of the word. She could feel herself growing, almost expanding upward, as if by making this bold decision she was becoming the fullest version of herself.

She packed—which didn't take long, as all of her worldly possessions could fit in a single rucksack—and then she made her goodbyes to her parents. As eager as she was to go with Eliezer, to meet her future, she did cry on her mother's shoulder, and she nearly shook with grief as she took leave of her father.

To Laban, however, she merely nodded and began walking out the door.

"Who's going to fetch our water?" he wailed to her retreating back.

Rebecca paused, set down her things, and turned back to grab the nearest jug of water. Then she lifted it up to her shoulder, stalked over to her brother, and much to his shock, and hers, dumped the whole thing over his head.

"Oh dear," she said, mocking his playful faux innocence. "I suppose you'll have to find someone soon."

And then she was gone, off on an adventure that would encompass a beloved husband, two children, and many, many a full belly and cheered heart at Rebecca's table.

CHAPTER FIVE

Sisters Stick Together

SEVEN YEARS AND ONE WEEK EXACTLY HAD PASSED SINCE Jacob, son of Isaac and Rebecca, had come to Haran and he and Rachel, daughter of Laban, had fallen in love at first sight. For one week now, Jacob had been pushing Laban every night at the dinner table to finally, finally let him marry Rachel. And every day, Rachel had been pushing Jacob to push some more. That was starting to annoy Jacob a little, but when she gave him a smile, he still looked at her as if the stars shone out of her eyes.

Tonight Rachel was hovering by the men's dinner table, fussing with the serving dishes, pouring more wine, making eyes at Jacob. Because of the veil covering Rachel's face and Laban's general inattention, her father didn't realize it was her, but Jacob knew. And, with her silent encouragement, Jacob was pressing him again. "You promised seven years, Laban. It's been seven years."

"She's too young."

I am not, Rachel thought.

"She is not," Jacob said. "She was not too young even seven years ago, and now if we wait much longer, she will be too old." Rachel stamped her foot softly and glared at Jacob. He winked at her. She suppressed a giggle.

"We can wait until after the sheep shearing," Laban said.

"That's four months from now," Jacob replied. Then he paused and gathered himself. Rachel had seen him at the marketplace, seen him negotiating with other herders, seen him managing the men who worked for her father. That look meant he was about to make the winning argument. "It would be terrible if, after all the work we've done to ensure your name is considered trustworthy in Haran, you were said to be breaking promises."

Rachel cheered in silence. The truth was, "we" hadn't done anything to create a trustworthy name for Laban; Jacob had done it all. Laban was always looking for an angle, for a trick, for a way to take advantage. Jacob's honesty and fair dealings had repaired all the damage Laban had done to his own reputation. It was a solid tactic for Jacob to take.

Sure enough, Laban rose from his chair, his brows drawn, his shoulders clenched. He was angry, but Rachel knew even before he spoke that they had won. "Fine," he spat out. "Rachel! Get in here!"

"I'm right here, Papa," she said, meek and demure, not pointing out that she'd been there the whole time and he hadn't noticed. The other women came in from behind the tent flap too. Rachel saw her older sister Leah and smiled broadly, flashing a quick thumbs-up.

"Oh. Good. Then you heard. You and Jacob will be married at the end of this week. And I don't want any arguments!" He pounded his fist on the table and stalked out.

As soon as he was out of earshot, everyone exploded with joy and laughter, clapping and cheering. Jacob and Rachel embraced; Jacob even spun her around in a circle while the gathered men and women hooted and hollered.

Leah cleared her throat. "A toast to the happy couple," she called, and she and some of the maids moved to refill everyone's wine cups. Toasts were made, more wine was drunk, and the celebrating lasted several hours more.

Rachel finally retired to the room she shared with Leah and found her sister sitting up, sewing something.

"Leah, you shouldn't sew by candlelight like this; you'll strain your eyes." She took the cloth out of Leah's hand, the veil Leah had been embroidering for Rachel on and off for the last seven years—the veil she'd wear at her wedding.

"I'm fine," she replied mildly. "My eye isn't bothering me today." Leah's right eye was milky and unsteady, the result of an accident when they were children. Well, the result of Laban's brutish carelessness. He probably hadn't thought about where the boiling water would land when he tossed that pot in anger. But he certainly hadn't cared enough to avoid splashing it in Leah's face. Nor had he taken care of the injury in a timely fashion so that it could heal.

Rachel fell back onto her pallet, kicking her sandals off as she did. "Can you believe it? Just four days and I can finally marry Jacob!"

Leah smiled. Mildly. Rachel detected a tear running down her cheek. "I wish you much love and good fortune, my dear sister," Leah said. "I hope you are happy in Beersheba. I'll miss you."

Rachel finally realized why her sister was upset. "Oh, no. Oh, Leah! I can't leave you here with... with him."

No need to qualify the "him." Their father was not particularly loving or attentive to Rachel, but it was nothing compared with the way he treated Leah. He would go out of his way to mock and belittle her or to give her the hardest tasks and then criticize how she performed them. And when he was in a rage, it was Leah who got caught by his fists or his feet.

But Rachel was terribly good at getting her way when she put her mind to something. "Well, there must be something we can do. Let me think."

"Don't do anything, Rachel, really. It's fine. I don't want you to throw away your chance for happiness."

"How can I be happy if I know I've made you miserable?" Rachel rolled to her side, hugging her sister quickly around the waist while also using her sister to stand herself up. "I'm going to go talk to Jacob. I think I have an idea."

"Rachel," Leah hissed. But Rachel was already half out the door, wrapping her scarf around her head.

Leah caught up with her a few feet away. "Rachel, you know I'm the one who'll get in trouble if you're sneaking out to meet your boyfriend. And please don't get me embroiled in whatever scheme you're cooking up."

"Quiet, Leah, we'll be heard," Rachel admonished with a little grin. Leah glared but quieted and followed her out.

Rachel found Jacob with the sheep, getting them settled in for the night. He lit up when he saw her but refrained from any embarrassing displays of affection when he saw Leah was with her. "Good evening, Leah," he greeted her, and then his eyes darted between the two sisters. "What are you up to?"

Rachel gave him an impish smile. "Why would we be up to anything?"

"When aren't you?" he replied, gazing at her fondly, until Leah cleared her throat.

"Honestly, you two."

Jacob shrugged and wrapped an arm around Rachel's shoulders. "What can I say? We're in love."

Rachel snuggled herself under his arm and grasped his hand. "We are, my angel. But listen. We can't leave my sister here. With him."

Rachel looked up at Jacob, and not surprisingly to her, he immediately nodded. "I've been worrying about that. Do you think your father will let her come with us? If we say you need her as a companion?" He stroked Rachel's hair. "Since you're so, you know, young and all?"

Rachel swatted him, but Leah was already shaking her head. "No. Not a chance. He needs me here."

"You definitely keep this household together," Jacob said, which was both kind and an understatement.

"I think you have to marry her, Jacob," Rachel said.

Leah's jaw dropped. But Jacob looked as if it had already crossed his mind too. "I won't give you up, Rachel," he said.

"I know, I know. I'm not saying marry her instead of me; I'm saying marry her *and* me." Seeing their skeptical faces, she said, "It's not like he'd be the first man around here with more than one wife."

"That's usually really wealthy men, though," Leah said.

"Yes, and Jacob has made our family so much wealthier," Rachel said. "Which is why Father can't afford to make Jacob really mad. I'm thinking we get Father to pull a trick. Or at least get him to think he's pulling a trick. We replace me with Leah as the bride. It's pretty easy to do if we have Leah wear the veil she made for me; no one will see our faces. Then you can pretend to be surprised and outraged when you realize the trick, but by then it's too late! You're married. Then to save face, he'll have to give you me too, because he won't want to seem like he pulled out of the deal."

Leah had now been stunned into silence. Jacob nodded. "But how do we get him to think it's his idea?"

Rachel peeked up at Jacob nervously. "I was thinking of letting one of the men overhear Leah complaining about her little sister getting married first, how it should be her, how the first child is entitled to certain rights." She cringed a little bit. Jacob, after all, had usurped his own older brother's rights, pretending to be Esau to steal their father Isaac's final blessing. But this area of sensitivity for Jacob was exactly why her father would take the bait.

He nodded, a little stiffly, but then he squeezed Rachel's shoulder and she smiled. "Leah?" Jacob looked at her with concern. She hadn't spoken or even moved in a while. "Leah, I know it's unusual for a shepherd like me to have more than one wife, but I think we can make this work." He reached for her hand. "My mother would be disappointed in me, I think, if I left you here with him." For a moment, Rachel had forgotten that Jacob's mother, Rebecca, had also grown up in this house. She had surely known her share of Laban's meanness.

Leah finally blinked, staring deeply at Jacob first and then studying her sister's face. Rachel made sure there was nothing to see there but encouragement.

Finally Leah relaxed, squeezed Jacob's hand, and leaned against Rachel, nuzzling her head affectionately. "This is going to be pretty strange," she said, "being married to my sister's husband. But I'll be happy to stay with you always, Rachel. And Jacob, thank you. This is a true kindness."

"Not at all," he said, smiling reassuringly. "I have seen how well you manage all of us in your father's household. You are the kind one for agreeing to come along."

And so they put their plan in motion. Leah complained, loudly, in a few different places, sure that one of the people whose ears her complaints reached would report them to her father. There was always a trouble-stirrer or two in Laban's tents. Her father did, indeed, the day of the wedding, call both of the girls in and announce with a flourish that Leah would take Rachel's place. Leah pretended to be dismayed, and Rachel gave an excellent impression of being distraught, which only made their father happier about "his" plan.

The following morning, Jacob stormed out of the wedding tent and hollered at Laban, who was at the breakfast table, surrounded by his men and many of their neighbors and friends. Laban laughed and needled Jacob about second-born children, but of course, to make sure it didn't look as if he were reneging on a promise, he said Jacob could marry Rachel the following week.

The only wrinkle was that Laban insisted on another seven years of labor from Jacob. The girls grumbled. Jacob considered it his due for playing a trick on another family member. But these seven years were better. As Jacob's wife, Leah was protected from the worst of her father's behavior. And soon, she and Rachel had a pile of children—playful, clever, joyful children who required a great deal of their attention and brought them a great deal of delight. Jacob said that God had promised his grandfather Abraham that his descendants would form a great nation. As Rachel gazed with joy on Jacob's many children, she felt sure that this promise was well on its way to fulfillment.

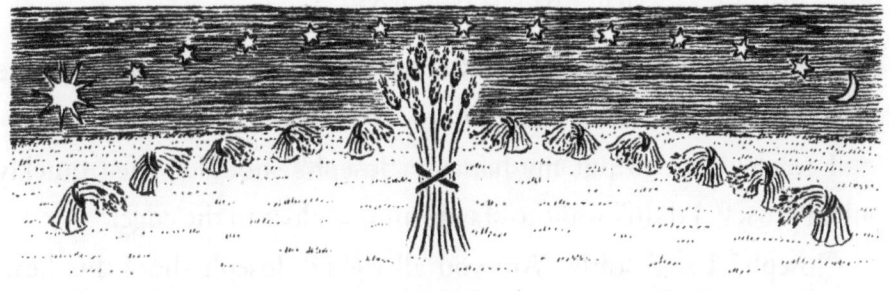

CHAPTER SIX

Standing at the Edge of the Pit

MY FAMILY HAD BEEN LIVING IN EGYPT FOR SEVENTEEN years when my father died. But he had insisted that we bury him in Canaan. My older brothers and I made the journey together, crossing the land where we'd grazed our cattle before the famine—the land where I had long believed my brother Joseph had died.

But there we were, all twelve of us together again in Canaan, honoring our father like a normal family. As if we hadn't been separated for so many years. As if our family had never been torn apart by lies and betrayal.

We were halfway back to Egypt when Joseph suddenly came to a stop. He stood silently at the edge of a pit; his shoulders were hunched, his expression unreadable.

I didn't know how Joseph could tell this pit from any of the dozens like it that dotted the landscape. But as I drew closer, something in the air seemed to shift. It felt colder where my brother was standing.

I reached out to put my hand on Joseph's shoulder, then quickly pulled it back. I didn't want to startle him, so close to the edge.

"Joseph," I said softly. "Are you all right?" Joseph shook his head slightly but didn't turn around. "What happened here? You can tell me anything, you know."

"Leave me alone, Benjamin." Joseph lifted his hand in a dismissive wave. "Please."

I slunk back to where our ten brothers were gathered. Half-brothers—Joseph was my only full brother. Like me, they were staring at Joseph as he stood over the pit. They didn't seem to notice my approach.

"He remembers," Judah murmured.

"Of *course* he remembers!" Reuben hissed back. "Would you forget your brothers throwing you in a pit and leaving you for dead?"

"We took him out," said Judah.

"To sell him to traders!" Reuben's voice grew louder. "He could have died in Egypt."

"But he didn't," said Judah quietly.

"Thank God," said Reuben. "That was a miracle."

My brothers murmured in agreement. *A miracle.* For all that my brothers had teased Joseph for his grandiose dreams, he *did* seem to be a person to whom miracles happened. He was also a person who tended to get into the kind of trouble that required miracles to get out of.

Judah looked at Reuben. "Do you think he really forgives us?"

"I don't know," Reuben shrugged. "Would you?"

I cleared my throat, and Reuben jumped, bringing their conversation to an abrupt end. They always seemed to fall quiet around me. I was never entirely sure what they had done to Joseph all those years ago. I had been too young to understand. I was only, just now, beginning to piece the story together.

One day I had a brother, and the next day he was gone.

It might have had something to do with the coat my father had bought for Joseph. Jacob had always favored our mother, Rachel. When she died, just after I was born, our father transferred his affection onto Joseph. He gave Joseph gifts to let him—and everyone who met him—know who was Jacob's favorite.

This coat was embroidered in the finest threads dyed in the rarest, and most expensive, colors. Flaming red. Deep-sea blue. Royal purple. It was not the kind of coat worn by a shepherd. From the moment Joseph put it on, it was clear that he didn't plan on being a shepherd for long.

Joseph's dreams only made things worse. Each morning, he'd run out from his tent, his coat flying like eagles' wings behind him, shouting, "I had the most incredible dream."

Our half-brothers did not find the dreams incredible. I couldn't blame them. Every dream was the same as the one before it. Sometimes we were stars; sometimes sheaves of grain. But in every dream, my brothers and I bowed down to Joseph.

"Bowing down to him!" Asher huffed one morning. "Can you believe him?"

"I'm surprised his sheaf of grain wasn't wearing a fancy little jacket," muttered Gad.

"We should tear off the sleeves and shove them down his throat." Simeon laughed. "That might shut him up."

"He'd never *dream* that was coming!" Levi added, and the two of them dissolved in laughter.

But it didn't sound like they were joking.

Even though I knew our other brothers found him irritating, I idolized Joseph the way little brothers do. Our brothers saw this as me taking sides, and they shut me out and shooed me away whenever they could. I was still a young boy, maybe ten years old, so most days, when they took our flocks out to graze, they left me behind.

One morning, our father sent Joseph to check on our brothers, even though Jacob knew his other sons hated it when Joseph tattled on them.

I should have been excited when Joseph asked me if I wanted to tag along, but I said no. I've always wondered if things might have turned out differently if I'd gone with him.

At sundown, the rest of my brothers returned, holding Joseph's coat—or what was left of it. The garment was torn to shreds and soaked in blood. Judah held up the tattered, bloody scraps to Jacob. "Do you recognize this?"

Jacob crumpled and cried out, "Joseph's coat! A wild animal has devoured him!"

Jacob was crying too hard to see the look that passed between my brothers: Guilt. Shame. And maybe, I wondered, relief?

I thought back to Simeon threatening to shove Joseph's coat sleeves down his throat. Is that what they'd done?

But the thought quickly passed as I ran to my father's side. Holding the bloodstained pieces of fabric, he howled as if it were his own heart that was torn in two.

I would have thought that my brothers would have been happier with him gone. But now, whenever something went wrong, my brothers had no one to blame but themselves—and each other.

As it turned out, getting rid of Joseph hadn't lightened our workload or earned us any more of our father's affection. Jacob seemed to age thirty years overnight, and he shuffled around like a ghost. What little energy he had, he poured into protecting me from harm.

"You are all that remains of my beloved Rachel," he'd say whenever I wanted to do anything remotely fun or adventurous. "I need you by my side."

I thought my brothers would turn on me as they had turned on Joseph, now that I was technically the favorite. But all I saw in their eyes was pity. Pity and guilt.

My brothers never spoke Joseph's name in my presence. But once in a while I overheard them talking about what had happened.

"Didn't I tell you not to hurt the boy?" said Reuben. "This drought is our punishment."

"We didn't hurt him," Judah corrected. "We sold him. Whatever happened to him afterward was not our fault."

"How long did you think he'd last?" Reuben said. "He'd never worked a day in his life!"

"Whose fault is that?" Judah snickered. "I bet his masters didn't find his dreams amusing, either."

My brothers would fall silent immediately if they caught me listening. I learned that it was useless to ask questions. But sometimes, I could see that my brothers were thinking about what they'd done.

Once I caught Judah looking at our father with tears in his eyes. In these lean years of famine, we'd all grown thinner. But Jacob was wasting away. Even when we put food in front of him, he barely tasted it. He walked hunched over like a much older man.

"I thought we were getting rid of Joseph," I heard Judah say, almost to himself. "I didn't think we'd be losing our father too."

When the drought turned to famine, my father sent my brothers to buy food in Egypt. I made every possible argument as to why they should take me with them. But my father didn't want me to leave, and my brothers didn't want me to come along.

My brothers were gone for longer than we expected. When they returned, there were only nine of them. They looked as if they'd seen a ghost.

"Pharaoh's chief adviser accused us of spying!" Reuben said.

"He took Simeon hostage," added Judah. "He ordered us to bring him our youngest brother."

My heart began to pound. For a moment, I thought my brothers were lying again. I wondered what Simeon had done to earn their wrath and if this was a plan to get rid of me too. But when everyone looked at me, I realized that they were telling the truth.

Jacob burst into tears. "Why did you tell him you had another brother?"

"They say he has the gift of prophecy," said Judah. "He must have known we were hiding something."

"If I lose Benjamin..." Jacob shook his head, as if I were still a child and not nearly twenty.

"Father!" I spoke up. "We need to get Simeon back. We need more food or all of us will die. Please...let me go."

Jacob buried his face in his hands.

It was Judah who spoke. "I promise, I will bring him back to you. Or we won't come back at all."

Jacob didn't look up, but waved us off as if to say, *Fine, go.*

Though he was clean-shaven and wore the clothes of Egyptian nobility, I recognized Joseph right away. It was like looking in a mirror. We both had our mother's face, or so I was told. How had my brothers missed it?

I could tell that Joseph recognized us too, as the brothers who'd betrayed him so long ago. People had been hiding things from me my whole life. I could easily spot a liar.

I went along with Joseph's game, even when he accused me of stealing his silver goblet and threatened to throw me in jail. Maybe this was his plan to keep me with him. But couldn't he see how much that would hurt our father?

I never imagined that my brothers would come to my defense. "If you take one of us," Judah said, "you must take all of us. He's our brother. We are responsible for him."

"I only want the thief," Joseph sneered. "I have no use for the rest of you."

"Please." Judah threw himself at Joseph's feet. "I promised my father I'd protect him. We lost his brother long ago, and it was all my fault. Take me instead."

Silence fell over the room, broken only by Joseph's weeping. The sobs shook his whole body. For a long time he could not speak at all. Finally, he took a breath.

"I am Joseph, the brother you sold." His voice was ragged with tears. "Tell the truth—is our father still alive?"

At first our brothers glanced at each other sideways, as if they thought this was another trap. I watched their faces closely as it dawned on them, one by one, that Joseph was telling the truth, a truth even more frightening than when they thought he was about to take one brother hostage. Whatever they had done to Joseph long ago, this was his chance to take revenge on all of them. One by one, our brothers fell to their knees, weeping and begging for mercy.

But Joseph's voice was soft, filled with more kindness than I ever would have expected. "You thought you were sending me to my death. But God had other plans. If you hadn't sold me to Egypt, we all would have died in the famine. But here, I've helped Pharaoh to prepare rations to last us for years. God sent me ahead of you, so that I could save all of our lives."

My brothers' mouths hung open in shock. I couldn't tell whether they were more stunned by Joseph's revelation or by his compassion.

"I'm sorry that I tested you," Joseph said. "I can see now that you have changed. You stood up for each other. You took care of each other. And I promise to take care of you too. Now please, tell me." He looked at me. "Is our father still alive?"

Unable to speak, I nodded. Joseph opened his arms wide, and I fell into them. One by one, my brothers joined our embrace.

When we returned home and told Jacob that Joseph was alive, he shouted, "Take me to Egypt! I must see Joseph before I die!" And once we were settled in Egypt, it was as if Jacob became a young man again. He died only recently, after seventeen happy years with his favorite son, with all of his children and grandchildren gathered around him for a blessing.

For years after we had settled in Egypt, I had wanted to ask Joseph how he really felt, if he'd really forgiven our brothers or if he ever got angry about it. But I was always afraid to bring it up. The unspoken agreement was that it was better not to talk about it.

But now, at this field in Canaan, the subject had come up of its own accord. We had literally stumbled upon it.

I turned to go comfort Joseph, but Judah stepped forward first. He stood beside Joseph for a long time, staring into the pit.

"It's deeper than I remember it," Joseph said.

"Darker too," said Judah. "You must have been so scared."

Our brothers began to look nervously at one another. The same thought had clearly crossed all of their minds at once. Now that our father was dead, what was to stop Joseph from finally taking his revenge?

"Our father would have wanted for you to forgive us…" Zebulon's trembling voice pierced the charged silence. "He told us himself before he died…"

"No more lies!" Judah interrupted. "Joseph, what we did to you was the worst thing we could have done. We would understand if you wanted to hurt us."

"Or if you made us your slaves," added Reuben. "It would only be fair."

But if we were really going to talk about fair, we couldn't rule out the possibility of Joseph tossing our brothers into the pit, one by one, and leaving them there. Or selling them off to traders. That's what I would have done—what any of us might have done if we'd been in the same position. Being slaves in the palace was too good for them.

Maybe there was something special about Joseph, though. He turned to face us, his face streaked with tears. "Is that why you think I stopped?"

"Isn't it?" Simeon asked. "This is where it all began."

"This is where my life was saved," Joseph corrected. "This is where my path, our path, changed forever. If it hadn't happened, I might still be the snotty little brother who boasted about his dreams. I wouldn't be who I am if not for what happened that day in this pit." He swiped at his tears with the back of his hand. "Neither would any of you. Now we really know what it means to love and take care of our brothers, because we know what it means to lose one."

I had to admit that he was right. Losing Joseph and finding him again had taught us what it meant to be brothers to each other. Judah would never have stood up for me had he not carried so much regret for what he'd done to Joseph.

"I know it's hard to believe," Joseph continued, "but I really did forgive you back in Egypt."

"Then why would you ever want to visit this terrible place again?" asked Reuben. "And why are you crying?"

"Father once told me that there was a blessing for everything," Joseph said softly. "Even for being saved from danger. When I saw the pit again, I wanted to say that prayer here." Joseph's tears began to flow once again down his cheeks. "But I can't remember the words he taught me."

Judah took Joseph's hand, and our brothers followed, making a circle around the pit. Judah whispered the words into Joseph's ear, and Joseph repeated them: "Blessed be this place, where God performed a miracle for me."

"And blessed be this place," Judah added, "where we are all together again, without anger, or fighting, or jealousy." And all of us said *amen*.

We stayed beside the pit for a long time, standing close to one another, until the sun sank low in the sky and it was time for us to make camp. I looked one more time at my brothers, standing together in the fading light.

I wish our father could have seen us.

CHAPTER SEVEN

A Matter of Life and Death

I don't know why Hebrew babies were always born at night. Maybe they knew that even midwives like Puah and I spent our days collecting straw and making bricks with the rest of the slaves.

Or maybe they came at night because that's when they thought they could hide from Pharaoh.

It was no secret that our people were growing in number. Rumors spread through the camp that Pharaoh wanted to put a stop to it. He increased our workload, making our days so exhausting and unbearable that it was hard to imagine adding new life to our families.

But somehow new life found a way. Most nights, as soon as I lay my head down on the cool mud floor, my limbs like wet sand, I'd hear footsteps outside my door, and I'd grab my supplies before I even heard anyone knocking. Most mornings, just before dawn, I'd lay a newborn safely in its mother's arms, then run back home to steal a few moments of sleep before the day's work began.

It was on one of these early mornings that I woke to thumping on my door. "Shifra, midwife to the Hebrews!" a man's voice bellowed. Heart pounding, I threw open the door. This wasn't a typical summons.

The glint of sun against the soldier's shield nearly blinded me as he spoke again. "Come with me. Pharaoh wishes to speak with you." He stepped aside so I could see that Puah stood, trembling, behind him. "Both of you."

Pharaoh was pacing the floor when we arrived, muttering to himself so intently that I thought he hadn't heard us come in.

"You sent for us, Your Highness?" I tried to sound polite, but official. "We're the midwives for the Hebrew women."

"The Hebrew women are like animals!" Pharaoh's voice was so loud that Puah jumped. I winced at his cruel words. "No matter how much I increase their workload, they keep having babies!"

There wasn't much we could say to that. Pharaoh was right, and we had the sleepless nights to prove it.

"It has been a fertile time for our people," Puah offered.

"What a blessing that there will be so many more Hebrews to build your great cities." I practically choked on the words. Every time we helped a woman give birth, we were giving Pharaoh another slave. It broke my heart.

"I can't risk having foreigners outnumber us," Pharaoh countered. "You must help me put a stop to this."

"Us?" My stomach dropped. "But what can *we* do?"

Pharaoh turned to look us squarely in the eyes. "When you assist the Hebrew women, as soon as you see that the child is a boy, kill it."

Puah gasped. "And what if it's a girl?"

"If it's a girl…?" He waved the question away, as if it didn't matter one way or the other. "Let her live. The Hebrew women are no threat to us. Women can be easily overpowered."

I knew that even one question might cost us our lives, but I couldn't help myself. "But why would someone as powerful as you be afraid of a few baby boys?"

"Boys grow into men," Pharaoh replied. "They become soldiers, rebels, and spies."

"But you have soldiers and taskmasters set over the Hebrews by the hundreds," Puah added. "Why ask us for help?"

"The women trust you," Pharaoh shrugged. "You can make it look like an accident."

He was right. Babies often died during childbirth or soon afterward. They were so fragile and weak. It wouldn't have been difficult to follow Pharaoh's orders without drawing attention to ourselves. But we had spent our entire lives protecting women and their babies. How could we even think of killing them?

Pharaoh's sharp voice interrupted my thoughts. "I order you to do this for me." He started pacing again. "I will reward you with great wealth, easier tasks for you and your families. But if you refuse—it is *your* lives that I will end."

We walked most of the way back in stunned silence. Stealing a sideways glance at Puah, I saw tears streaming down her face. The lump in my throat was so thick that I didn't know if I would be able to speak. But as we drew closer to home, my words came tumbling out. "What are we going to do?"

Puah stopped walking. "I don't know..." Her voice was more forceful than I expected. "But we cannot do what he said."

"How can we disobey him?" My words choked me. "He could put us to death!"

"How can we betray the trust of our women like that?" Puah responded sharply. "How can we murder the children we've always protected?" Her voice caught on the word "murder."

"He'll notice that the Hebrew women keep having babies," I pointed out. "What will we tell him then?"

"We'll have to think of something," Puah said. "It's a matter of life and death."

In the week that followed, five days passed without a birth, something we had not experienced since we first began our work as midwives. It was as if our babies had sensed the danger and decided not to be born. Or perhaps their mothers had heard of our meeting with Pharaoh and decided not to summon us.

Puah and I didn't chatter in the fields or sleep in shifts as we had done before. I was so used to being awakened late at night that no matter how exhausted I was, I couldn't fall asleep. I sat up each night, replaying our conversation with Pharaoh and mine with Puah. I waited for the birth that would tell me whether I was a midwife or a murderer, a traitor or a trickster. I asked myself who I was most afraid of: God, Pharaoh, or myself?

I could not imagine following Pharaoh's orders. But I worried for myself and Puah and for our families. What kind of punishment would Pharaoh inflict upon us if we refused? What would become of the women we served if we were killed? If we didn't obey Pharaoh's orders, couldn't he easily replace us with midwives who would?

Maybe if we obeyed and fewer boys were born, Pharaoh would leave the rest of the Hebrews alone. Was it worse for a mother to believe that a child had been stillborn or to have that child rounded up later by Pharaoh's soldiers? Could we justify following Pharaoh's orders if it prevented future pain?

On the sixth restless night after our meeting with Pharaoh, I lay awake, listening to nothing. Often the varied noises of our village woke me from my sleep, but now it was the silence that kept me awake.

Just when I began to think that the night would never end, I heard quick footsteps outside my house. As usual, I opened the door before I even heard a knock. There stood a young girl, her eyes wide with worry.

"It's my mother," she told me before I could ask. "She said it would be soon." The girl departed as quickly as she arrived. I had to run to keep up with her as she twisted and turned through a labyrinth of identical houses.

This is it, I thought. *Tonight I'll become either a murderer or a fugitive.* The sound of our quick steps shook the thought from my mind. When we reached the house, I burst through the door.

The young girl's mother lay in the corner of the house, her moans long and low, her nightdress soaked with blood. She looked and sounded like a wounded beast. I remembered how Pharaoh had called us animals.

But when the woman's eyes met mine, her face softening with relief, it was *my* animal instincts that kicked in. I didn't think about what I would do if the baby was a boy or how I'd answer to Pharaoh if I disobeyed him. I knelt beside the laboring woman, as close to her body as if it were my own, and did what I had always done. I rubbed her belly with soothing oils and murmured words of encouragement as her pains intensified. When it was time for her to push, I lifted her up so she could kneel over the birth bricks.

I don't remember seeing the baby emerge or feeling its delicate head slide into my waiting hands. I heard the child's cries as if from a distance as I rubbed its skin dry with salt, swaddled it in a cloth, and handed it to its mother.

I did not even think about whether it was a boy or a girl until the mother looked up at me and smiled. "Isn't he beautiful?" she asked.

I nodded. The baby gurgled as his mother drifted off to sleep. He *was* beautiful. All of our children were beautiful. And, as long as I could do anything about it, all of them would live.

When I saw Puah the next morning, she looked how I felt: frazzled and dirty, dizzy with fear.

"You too?" I asked.

She nodded. "A boy?" I nodded.

"Me too," she said.

We stood facing each other in silence, not wanting to ask the next question.

"How is he?" I finally asked.

"Healthy and strong." Puah smiled. "Eating like a wild animal."

It was as if her words had unlocked a secret compartment in my brain. "What did you just say?"

"He's eating like a wild animal," she repeated.

"That's it!" I grasped Puah's arm tightly. "I know what we can tell Pharaoh."

Even with our plan in place, we dreaded the summons from Pharaoh. But weeks later, when the messenger arrived, we made the long walk to the palace hand in hand.

Pharaoh didn't bother with a greeting. "Why have you done this?" he shouted at us. He launched right into an attack. "How could you let the boys live?"

Puah and I stared at the floor, waiting for Pharaoh to say the magic word.

"Was there no way to stop them?" Pharaoh roared. "How is it that they continue to multiply like animals?"

I looked at Puah. *Now.*

"Your Highness," she began, "you were absolutely right about the Hebrew women. They're not like the Egyptian women."

"That's right," I joined in. "They're like animals! Before we could even get to their homes, they had already given birth."

The silence that followed felt like an eternity. Puah and I held our breath as Pharaoh considered our excuse. He looked perplexed, as if he were standing before the mighty Sphinx, instead of two lowly midwives.

Our lies made us nervous, even after weeks of rehearsing, because they sounded so ridiculous to us. But apparently they didn't sound that ridiculous to Pharaoh. For all his power and influence, there was one place he had never been. He had never crouched beside a woman as she gave birth to a child. That world was foreign to him. He had to rely on us to explain its mysteries. He'd said himself that Hebrews were different from Egyptians, that our women were like animals. We'd simply used his own words against him.

Finally Pharaoh shook his head and muttered, "How foolish I was to give this task to women!" He turned to us. "Go back home and never speak of this again."

"As you wish, Your Highness," we said at once, fleeing the palace as fast as our legs could take us.

We would be known among our people not for what we did, but for what we did not do, what we could not do. We were midwives. We'd devoted our lives to helping mothers and their babies. There was no part of us that could ever have put one of them in danger.

Even in our relief, Puah and I wondered why Pharaoh hadn't carried out his threat against us. Perhaps he'd simply had a change of heart, if he even had a heart to change. Or maybe he just hadn't seen us as a threat. We were only Hebrew women, after all.

CHAPTER EIGHT

Miriam Saves Her Brother

THINGS COULD ALWAYS GET WORSE, THAT MUCH MIRIAM knew. She was only a child, but she still spent her days hard at work. Sometimes she worked with her father in the mud pits, making brick after brick in the hot desert sun. Sometimes she worked with her mother, Yocheved, in the kitchens, where they'd prepare food and drink for all the workers on a site, twenty women shouting above her, boiling water sloshing and knives flashing. Sometimes she worked as a messenger for the Egyptians, running around the city all day long. Those were the best days. Those days were the closest to freedom that Miriam ever experienced. Pathetic, that "choose which alley to run down" or "choose to dawdle by the riverside for a moment" passed for freedom in Miriam's life, but Miriam knew enough not to take small pleasures for granted.

The old pharaoh hadn't really thought of the Hebrew slaves as people. They had just been the workforce, one more cog in the enormous machine that was the Egyptian empire. He gave the Egyptian taskmasters their orders—build this monument, repair this palace, clean these grain storage silos—and then let the taskmasters manage the slaves who would work on these projects. The taskmasters might whip you if they thought it would make you work harder. They preferred not to whip you too hard, because if you were maimed or even killed by the whip, you wouldn't be able to work. But if they did whip you hard enough to take you out of the workforce, your broken body would motivate the other slaves to work harder, so either way, the taskmasters got what they wanted. Miriam knew that the way the Hebrew slaves were treated wasn't, in any sense, good. But it could always get worse.

There'd been whispers when the new pharaoh was crowned. This new one *did* think of the Hebrew slaves as people, and he was afraid. He had apparently gotten a notion in his head that the Hebrew slaves might rise up against him. Apparently, freeing the slaves and letting them return to their homeland was not an option he considered to prevent an uprising. No, instead, allegedly, he'd ordered the Hebrew midwives to kill male babies as they were born. Then the midwives were supposed to tell the mothers that their babies had been stillborn.

Miriam didn't know if she believed that. She was too young to be involved in childbirth or even to have it openly discussed around her, but she could use her own eyes and ears. There had been babies born in the last few months, with the help of the midwives, and some of them were boys. If Pharaoh had given orders to the midwives, Miriam was certain they would have been followed. Her own mother had given birth to a baby boy only last week.

And there you had evidence that things could always get worse. Miriam already had an older brother, Aaron, who was as cranky and dour as one could wish. Adding an extra person to their already cramped quarters, another belly to fill with their already strictly rationed food, was definitely in the "worse" column, Miriam felt—even if this particular baby was pretty cheerful, and even though Miriam had to admit that he was pretty cute.

One morning, a few weeks after the extra belly was born, Miriam was pulled aside by the kitchen taskmaster and sent on a message-delivery errand. There couldn't be a better day for it. Miriam welcomed the opportunity to run around in the sun, exploring, meeting people. Maybe she'd even get a treat from an indulgent guard or maidservant. This morning she was sent to the palace gates first, which rarely yielded treats, but was impressive all the same.

A scribe stood with a pack of guards on the stairs, giving out scrolls. Miriam took the one intended for the guards of Goshen and dashed away. As soon as she was out of sight of the palace, she ducked into an empty alley and opened the scroll. She had been teaching herself to understand the funny pictures the Egyptians used for writing. She was getting pretty good at it. This appeared to be information about weaponry, which was odd. The Hebrew slaves usually didn't have anything to do with weaponry.

She heard heavy footsteps, clanging—Egyptian soldiers. She ducked deeper into the alley, into a crevice between two walls. Then she peered out.

One of the soldiers appeared angry. "This is what our training is for? We're soldiers. We're made for fighting the enemy in glorious battle, not slaughtering babies."

"The Lord of This World and The Next commands us—what else can we do?" the other replied, resigned.

The angry man's shoulders slumped. "We have no choice," he agreed.

No choice? Miriam huffed. What did these men know of no choice? They had swords and spears and shields, and training for battle. They were free Egyptian citizens. They were men. They had a whole host of options before them that others—

"So it's to Goshen then."

The first soldier grimaced at his friend. "Our spears will glisten with the blood of Hebrew babies." Then they disappeared around a corner.

Hebrew babies?!

Her brother!

Things could always get worse, but this was worse on a whole new level! Miriam may not have wanted a baby brother, but she certainly didn't want him killed!

She ran home to her mother. Miriam was always fleet of foot, but today she must have set speed records.

She tumbled into the house. "We need to hide the baby," she said, out of breath. Her mother looked at her, quizzical for a moment. Then she heard the stomping feet outside.

There was a deep indentation in the wall, where the stones had settled and created a little hole. Yocheved had kept chickens there, until they had needed to eat the chickens. It was lined with straw—good, soundproofing straw. Yocheved quickly created a bed for the sleeping baby in the wall with the straw and his blankets, and Aaron silently slid several bags of grain over the opening. The baby slept on. Safe.

Then the sound of a mother's scream was heard outside.

For the next few months, that sound filled the streets of Goshen. Women wept, wailed. Some of them flung themselves into the Nile. And when Miriam saw her own mother's face, terror and despair intermingled, she could hardly blame them.

One morning, Miriam was awakened well before dawn by her mother. Her mother held the baby to her breast, silencing him, and wordlessly nudged Miriam to get up and follow her.

Miriam's heart pounded as she snuck with her mother out of Goshen, tripping nimbly over the uneven stone and sand to the spot on the river just below town where the bank curved just so, so that they would not easily be seen by the guards in the tower.

Yocheved pulled out an object from the reeds. It was a basket, lined with worn straw and threadbare stretches of cloth. Miriam recognized the patterns on the cloth as belonging to the various Hebrew tribes' prayer shawls.

"Your brother's cries grow too loud," Yocheved said, her voice barely above a whisper, barely discernible over the rushing of the water past the reeds. "We won't be able to hide him much longer."

"So you're going to drown him?" Did "worse" know no limits?

Yocheved looked at her, horrified. "And do the soldiers' work for them? No. I'm sending him down the river." And Yocheved settled her sleepy baby in the basket. The baby looked up at them and smiled softly, that smile Miriam knew was a smile of love.

And perhaps a little gas. The distinct odor floated past them on the breeze.

"Wait, you're sending him down the river? In that basket?"

"Yes."

"*Ima*, that's... that's insane. You might as well drown him; he's going to die!"

"No. Our God will protect him. I have prayed it will be so."

"But... but... *Ima*, how will we know what becomes of him? If you put him in this basket, he is as lost to us as he would be if he were killed."

Her mother leveled a look at Miriam that pierced her heart. "He does not exist for us, Miriam. He exists for himself and for the world." She placed a gentle kiss on the baby's forehead and tucked him in. "Besides, you're going to follow the basket."

Miriam's face lit up with sudden understanding.

"Stay hidden in the reeds and report his fate to me as soon as you are able. If you come to a place where you cannot follow, then return quickly, and we will pray together. Don't let anyone see you." And with one motion, Yocheved settled a kiss on her daughter's brow and pushed her son's basket out into the flow of the Nile River.

Miriam scooted through the reeds. She was good at hiding, good at being quick and silent. And she'd spent many a resting day along this very river; she knew where the sand turned too marshy to walk and where the bank was visible to the passing Egyptians. She followed the basket swiftly as it crested over waves and dodged rocks and even made its way through a narrow passage between two boats, whose passengers fortunately didn't notice or care about a floating basket enough to inspect it. Miriam couldn't quite see the baby, couldn't tell if he was happy or scared or asleep, but she kept the basket in sight until the flow of the river took it past the sprawling white walls of the homes of the courtiers and approached the palace.

The palace. Oh dear. Miriam had trouble finding places to hide from the high windows. Sometimes she ducked underwater and hoped that if she was seen, she'd merely be mistaken for the shadow of a fish. Sometimes she just prayed and moved swiftly. No one was outside at the moment. No guards overlooked the river. They'd pass the palace by and be safe—soon.

Only they didn't pass it, not quite. Right behind the great walls of the palace, a channel had been dug, and the river flowed into a hidden grotto behind it. That was where the basket floated. Miriam tried to breathe slowly, carefully, quietly, but still her heart raced. She moved across the channel and hid herself in the reeds there.

The basket floated toward several women in white linen, splashing and laughing in the water. Their skin was clear and their hair was shining, and their hands looked as if they'd never done a day of hard labor. Miriam felt her bitter anger rising. How could there be Goshen, with its work-worn hands, its whip-injured backs, its starvation-decimated limbs, and only a short walk away, people living in such luxury? But now was not the time. She had to watch the basket.

The women noticed the basket. They looked curious, then soft and smiling—they must have seen her brother's face. It was quieter back here, and Miriam thought she could just hear the sound of her brother's coos.

The women beckoned, with their long, graceful arms, to someone just out of Miriam's sight. Then they shifted away from the basket as another woman, stately and spectacular and arrayed in finery, approached the basket.

The princess.

Miriam's heart sank like a stone to the bottom of the river. Pharaoh's daughter! Her brother would die for sure! Would the princess do it herself—throttle or drown him or dash him against the stone steps on which she had been lounging? Would she call for a guard? Or would she bring him to Pharaoh himself, to show how devious the Hebrews were in their efforts to evade his soldiers? Miriam began to dash toward the basket, but then two things she saw on the princess's face stopped her.

The first was a softening, just like the other women. She was charmed by the baby.

The second was a quick glance up, to where Miriam had just barely rustled the reeds. And then a quelling look, so quick it might have been a twitch, but a look that Miriam had seen on her mother's face a dozen times. *Stop*, the look said. *Just stay still and be quiet.*

So Miriam stayed still and was quiet.

That soft look returned to the princess's face, more exaggerated than before, and Miriam got the impression that she was performing for her servants. Miriam shifted just a bit, staying carefully hidden, so she could hear.

"The gods have delivered me a baby," the princess was declaring to her servants. "They have heard my grief for my late husband, and they have sent me this baby to comfort me!"

The young women surrounding her cooed and applauded. Some held out their arms to hold the baby, but the princess held him close to her.

An older woman, worn and plainly dressed, approached the princess's elbow. The attendants behind her had returned to their chatter and play and so could not hear her murmur to the princess, "Could that not be a Hebrew baby?" But Miriam could just barely hear the question, which was not really a question. The old woman pulled out one of the pieces of cloth. She must have known the pattern was a Hebrew one.

The princess barely glanced at the reeds before sending a sharp, angry look at the old woman. A quelling look, like the one she'd sent Miriam, the look that said, *Be quiet*—but with a lot more force. Then her face was sunshine again as she waved to the attendants behind her. "Go on, go inside," she told them. "I wish to enjoy my new darling's smiles alone."

The women left with much tittering and smiling and cooing at the baby. The old woman stayed at her mistress's elbow until the princess snarled, "You too." The older woman, clearly unhappy, turned and left.

Miriam watched the princess for a few minutes, cooing and fussing at her brother, tickling his toes and nuzzling his cheeks. Whatever act she was putting on for her attendants, she clearly was happy to have a baby arrive at her doorstep.

"You can come out of there, girl. I wish to speak to you," the princess called, and Miriam was startled to realize that the princess was addressing her.

Slowly Miriam crept out of the reeds, though she dared not approach too closely. Perhaps the princess would do away with her, instead of the baby. She'd be harder to drown, though; she could fight back. Miriam planted her feet hard in the riverbed and stopped out of arm's reach of the princess.

The princess didn't seem to mind. She didn't take her eyes off the baby, really. She just said, quite plainly, "Can I assume that your mother is available to nurse this baby?"

Miriam swallowed hard. Her toes shifted the sand as she tried to work out what was happening here. The way the princess asked her question, the way she'd responded to her older attendant, she must know, mustn't she? She must know where this baby came from.

"Yes," Miriam said, a frog stuck in her throat.

The princess gave a short nod. "Go fetch her. She will stay in the palace as my servant and tend to this baby for me."

Miriam turned to go, still unable to process all that had happened. But a few feet away, she turned. The princess was still cooing and singing to her brother.

"Princess—, I—, you—"

"I really did want a baby," she answered, almost to herself. "I will be happy to have him here." She lifted him out of the basket then, held him aloft, and smiled at him. The baby smiled back. Miriam felt a stab of jealousy. "I shall call him Moses," the princess said. Another small surge of jealousy, that this Egyptian princess should have the privilege of naming Miriam's baby brother, Yocheved's son. But as long as he stayed alive, it hardly mattered.

Miriam could think of nothing more to say. She ran home, almost heedless of the possibility of being seen. Her head was too full of thoughts. She thought about the princess, who would be knowingly defying her father, right under his nose, for all of her baby brother's life maybe. She thought about the old servant, who seemed ready to serve the princess first, even if it meant disobeying Pharaoh's orders. And Miriam thought about the soldiers, who wouldn't defy Pharaoh, even with swords in hand. The midwives... maybe that rumor had been true. She thought about her mother, who'd sent her own son down the river, with only a prayer for his safety. And she thought about herself, how she'd successfully snuck past guards and kept her brother safe despite all the forces lined up against them.

Her mother was waiting for her at the door of their hovel. Miriam could not stop her face from breaking into a smile, and Yocheved nearly fainted in relief. Miriam related all that had happened.

Yocheved sent up a cry of joy and a prayer of thanks to God. She rushed to bundle her things to take to the palace with her.

"Is the princess powerful enough to defy Pharaoh?" Miriam asked nervously.

Yocheved smiled a little. "Imagine if someone was both your father and, according to everyone around you, 'Lord of This World and The Next.' Would you be eager to openly defy him?"

Yes, thought Miriam. She liked to imagine that if she were anything other than a slave, if she had any power at all, she'd use all of it to defy everything and everyone, to yell and scream and fight and bring the whole thing—what thing, she didn't know, but the whole of it—crashing to the ground.

But maybe there were other kinds of defiance. She thought about the way she helped her mother sneak her baby brother through the streets, the way she darted through reeds and hid underwater.

She thought of the way the princess had looked her servant in the eye and made clear that she was defying her father and that the servant had better do so too.

"She'll be bringing up a Hebrew boy under his very nose," Yocheved continued. "She'll be using her own position as princess to save the life of one her father wanted dead. That is how she is defying him, and it is brave of her. And she is kind enough to let me in, to let me be with my own child for as long as she can. It is enough. *Dayeinu.*"

Miriam wondered if it was enough and then wondered if it was even too much. Then she wondered what she would see when she saw her brother again. Things could always get worse, yes, she knew that. But maybe things could also get better.

CHAPTER NINE

Moses Sees

EVERY MORNING MOSES AWOKE WITH A DEEP SENSE OF gratitude and joy. He was grateful to still be alive. He was joyful that he had a wife he loved and a baby son they loved together. He was joyful that he was a part of a tribe, and an important, useful part too. His father-in-law, Jethro, was the chief, and his wife, Tzipporah, would be chief after him. He was grateful to have found his skill at shepherding, especially since his tribe relied on their sheep and goats for food, milk, warmth, and barter.

Sometimes Moses would remember the days when he'd been a prince in the palace in Egypt. He had been joyful then too. Joy had always come easy to him. But he had not been grateful. He had not even been aware of what a blessed life he led or what his manifold blessings cost others.

But that was in the past. He now leaned on a community, to be sure, but they leaned on him too. It filled him with pride to be useful, to be trusted, to be necessary.

So when the sunlight filtered through the threadbare tent, slanting over Moses's eyes, he woke with a prayer in his heart. *Thank You, God of the Mountains, God of the Ancestors, God of All That Is, for making me and bringing me here.* It was a standard form of prayer that he'd heard from Jethro's lips a million times. He was glad to have a way to express his gratitude.

When it was time to bring the sheep up to the grassy plateau of the mountain on which they were camped, Moses approached the makeshift fencing where he'd penned them for the night. The young ones, not quite adults yet, were already awake and tumbling noisily with each other. Moses took his staff from the side of the fence and rapped it on the ground, not too hard, but enough that the gamboling goats stopped their fighting for a moment and looked up. Then they barreled over to the fence, knocking each other around to get Moses's attention. Moses chuckled and held out the dried figs he carried as treats, making each of them stand still and separate from the other before offering a fig.

There were a few mother goats still nursing; their faces clearly communicated how little they wanted to get up and move their sleeping babies. So Moses entered the enclosure and knelt by them, gently scratching their heads, stroking the babies' backs until they were all awake and ready for the day. Slowly, slowly, with a treat here, a calming stroke, or a bit of playful tumbling, all of his charges were up and ready. The last one, the oldest, was stubborn. He insisted on wandering around the enclosure for a bit, nipping at some of the other goats, and finally lying back down at the gate. Moses tied a long stick of dried honey to the end of his staff and coaxed the old goat out of the enclosure by allowing him a lick every few steps.

And so Moses and his goats went up to the grassy plateau above their camp. The sun had not yet heated this plateau, so Moses lay down against a rock while his goats ate their fill. As the warmth of the sun started to turn to heat, he rapped his staff again. This time the goats, content with their meal, hurried into line to follow him down. The old goat walked by his side, as if he were as much the shepherd as Moses was, which made Moses smile.

As they turned a particularly shadowed corner, Moses saw something—something bright white and flickering—in a crevice. What could it be? He peered inside.

"Tch, tch," he said to the goats, which they knew meant "stay here." He squeezed himself through the crevice and found himself in a gorge. In the center of that gorge, a bush was aflame with an unnaturally white fire.

Moses stood for a moment, captured by awe. The fire crackled and flickered and sparked, but the branches it surrounded remained sturdy and strong, stretching and twisting themselves up toward the heavens. Moses was only feet from the fire, but he felt no heat, only a calm, soothing cool. He held his hand out, closer and closer to the bush. But the fire did not catch him. He brought his un-singed hand close to his face, turned it over and over, unable to believe that the wonder before him could be real. He let out a long breath into the cool, sweet air.

Though nothing appeared to move, it seemed to Moses as if the bush turned toward him. Then a voice issued from the bush. No, not exactly from the bush. The voice seemed to come from inside of Moses himself. It breathed his name, low and deep. "Moses," the Voice said, and Moses uttered a word he would have sworn he'd never heard in his life, but still it came from his lips: *Hineini*, "Here I am," in a tongue

Jethro would later tell him was an ancient one. *Hineini* was a promise to the God of the Mountains, a promise to serve that God in whatever way one could.

"Remove your shoes," the Voice said, "for the ground you stand upon is holy."

My shoes? Moses thought. It seemed an odd, seemingly unimportant command. Still, Moses was awed by this miracle of fire and this divine voice speaking inside him, so he swiftly followed it.

"Moses," the Voice continued. Moses resisted the urge to repeat that strange word *hineini* again. He just listened. "My people suffer, Moses. You must bring my people Israel out of Egypt, Moses. You must lead them to the land I have promised them, a land flowing with milk and honey. You must bring them out of slavery."

Slavery. The people of Israel. The people whose slavery had provided the luxury and comfort he had enjoyed as a child, while they suffered, and while their suffering barely entered his mind. The people who were his people too.

"Yes, Moses," said the Voice. "Yocheved, your nurse, was also your mother in truth. Miriam, who helped care for you, is your sister. I helped them save you from Pharaoh's bloody sword. I kept you safe, so that one day you could lead your people out."

Moses had known. He had *known*. And yet he had refused to know. Refused to see his eyes reflected to him in the eyes of his mother, his hair and his hands like his sister's, the love they showed him that was greater than the love of the other nursemaids for their charges. He had preferred being a prince—until he could not be a prince any longer.

Until that day when he had seen—seen exactly what his princely life cost *his* people. He had seen a taskmaster beat an elderly slave to death. He hadn't known what possessed him; the memory of it still made him want to vomit. But in his rage and disgust, he had taken that taskmaster's whip and killed the taskmaster.

That act, that vile act, was what led him here. To Midian.

To a bush that was afire but did not burn. To a voice that told him he had to go back.

"I cannot," he choked out first. Then he took a breath and reminded himself to address this divine voice more respectfully. "God of the Mountain, I thank you for saving me. I am honored that you would choose me for this task," he said gravely and formally, like an actor playing a part. "But I am the wrong person for this task. I am not capable of freeing Israel from Egypt."

"And yet I have chosen you," the Voice rang, in his head and all around the gorge. And then nothing—as if that should settle the matter.

But Moses could not fathom doing such a task. "I cannot appear before Pharaoh," he said, "as I am the murderer of an Egyptian. I cannot appear before the people of Israel either. Most of them do not know me, and those who do, know me as their oppressor. I have no army, no powers of persuasion, no reason for Pharaoh to listen to me, nor for the people of Israel to follow me." Still the Voice said nothing. "I can't even speak before Pharaoh. I have a stutter."

Finally the Voice spoke. "I will send your brother, Aaron, to you to help you. He is a good speaker."

"I have a brother?"

"Yes. Your parents' firstborn son. He's a Levite, a leader and a priest among the people already."

Moses rocked back on his heels. There was so much to process here. The feeling of dread in the pit of his stomach would not dissipate.

"How will I convince the people of Israel I speak for their—our—God? What will I tell them?"

"You will tell them that I am the God of your ancestors—God of Abraham and Sarah, of Isaac and Rebecca, of Jacob and Rachel and Leah. You will tell them that I have heard their cries and that I will do for them as I promised. I will set them free."

Abraham, Isaac, and Jacob; Sarah, Rebecca, Rachel, and Leah. Moses remembered these names, had heard them crooned in song by his nurse—his mother. So perhaps the people of Israel would believe him.

"Your sister, Miriam, will help you as well. She is the one who followed you down the river; she has always been your protector."

He remembered a sharp-eyed girl, watching his every move, moving rocks from his path and then chastising him for not being more watchful of them. But his mother—his princess mother, not his enslaved mother—would chuckle lightly, and Moses would laugh, never sensing that his life had ever been, or ever could be, in danger.

"What about Pharaoh? How will I convince him I speak for a God he's never heard of?"

"Cast your staff on the ground."

Moses glanced at his right hand, startled. He still held his shepherd's staff. What throwing it on the ground had to do with proving to Pharaoh that Moses spoke for the God of the Mountains—the God of the Ancestors—Moses did not know, but he threw it on the ground anyway.

Clearly, obeying confusing and nonsensical commands was going to be part of the job.

The staff turned into a snake. Moses gasped and jumped away, then felt a little embarrassed, as the snake seemed indifferent to him.

"Now grab it by the tail." Steeling himself with a deep breath, Moses did so. The snake was his staff again.

Moses knew he should look terribly impressed with this trick. But the truth was that Pharaoh wouldn't be. "If I might speak my mind, my God…" Moses waited. The Voice said nothing. The air in the gorge remained calm and still. "I know, of course, that my staff turning into a snake was a miracle from You. But this sort of trick is exactly what the magicians who come to Pharaoh's court do. They give the snakes potions to make them stiffen and relax. Pharaoh will think this is just a trick."

"He'll change his mind when I send My plagues."

"Plagues?"

"Plagues: Frogs, boils, locusts. Darkness and death. As many plagues as it takes to soften Pharaoh's heart. And after each one, you will demand once again that he let My people go."

The unease that had been roiling through Moses's stomach increased. He was expected to bring destruction to a people who had once been his? And why should the people of Israel trust him as a leader? After he had killed the taskmaster, he'd heard some Hebrew slaves whispering about it. Certainly it was no big loss to them if a particularly brutal taskmaster died. But if Moses could lose his temper so easily with an Egyptian, they had said, how easy would it be for him to lose his temper with a slave?

That had been the moment he'd decided to run away. Leave everything he'd ever known—his Egyptian palace, his family—and become someone else entirely.

He'd been so happy with this person he'd become. Now he was being told he would have to go back.

"God, I—"

"This is not for you to argue, Moses. I saved you so that you would be able to free My people, who suffer at the hands of the Egyptians. There is a job to do, and you must be the one to do it."

The people of Israel did suffer. And though he had not created their suffering, he had refused to see it for so long. He had refused to turn toward their suffering, to ease it. Now their suffering was his responsibility, and he had to end it.

Moses took a deep breath. He sighed heavily. Then he nodded in the direction of the bush.

The Voice came through him, soft and comforting. "You will have help, Moses. You will have your brother, Aaron, to help you speak, and your sister, Miriam, to help you lead. You will show My people that you can be of value to them, just as you showed Jethro and Tzipporah. You have shown that you are capable of leading a flock with compassion and kindness; you will now lead your flock, My people, through the wilderness. I will help you, Moses, and you will have My staff to perform My miracles."

Moses gripped the staff. It felt warm in his hand, in a way he hadn't noticed before.

"*Hineini*," he said to the Voice. *Here I am.*

CHAPTER TEN

Dancing on the Shores of the Sea

ON THE FIRST FULL MOON AFTER MY TWELFTH BIRTHDAY, my mother gently shook me awake.

"Come, Tehilah!" she whispered. "Don't wake your brothers."

Rubbing sleep from my eyes, I obeyed, following my mother as she tiptoed between my brothers' sleeping mats.

Outside, our neighborhood in Egypt was an upside-down version of the world we inhabited by day. Each morning, Hebrew men, women, and children trudged across the hot sand of Goshen, our sun-scorched shoulders already slumped in anticipation of the day's work.

Now, with the sky pitch-black against the cool glow of the moon, the ground was teeming with women and girls, their bodies lifted and light, as if they were floating just above the sand.

Just as I opened my mouth to ask, "What's happening?" I heard the steady beat of fingertips striking the smooth skin surface of a hand drum. Our steps fell in time with the rhythm as we moved toward the sound.

Turning a corner, I saw that the stream of women had stopped flowing forward. Now they moved in circles in a great pool of moonlight. In the center stood my grandmother, tapping out the beat on the leathery surface of a timbrel.

I'd never seen my grandmother play outside of our small mud house. She told me how her own great-grandmother had carried the timbrel with her all the way from Canaan, singing songs of hope, adventure, and new beginnings, back when Egypt was spread out before the starving Hebrews like a banquet of possibilities.

As the dream of life in Egypt crumbled into a nightmare, her grandmother hid the timbrel in our mud walls. If Pharaoh knew we had even this one simple pleasure, she worried, he would find a way to take it from us. But sometimes I could convince my grandmother to play for me.

Whenever her stiff fingers struck the drum, my tired body moved without thinking, swaying slightly to the beat, my aching arms stretching out overhead and turning in circles as the sound swelled.

Now I saw that others had kept their instruments too, long after everything valuable had been sold for grain or used to bribe a taskmaster. All around me, women were drumming in time to my grandmother's beat, joining the circle of dancers.

A melody rose up over the drumming. Someone called out a verse, and the women repeated it, splitting into harmonies. It felt as if our song could reach the moon itself.

God is my strength and my song. God will be my deliverance.

"Who is that singing?" I asked between verses.

"Miriam, daughter of Yocheved," my mother said. "She leads this celebration every month, like the generations of women before her."

I stared, puzzled at this joyful gathering of slaves. "What are we celebrating?"

My mother leaned in close to speak over the din. "That we can still make music. That we can still feel joy. And that even the Egyptians can't take those things away from us."

From that night on, I never missed a full-moon gathering. Even as Pharaoh increased our burdens and exhaustion seeped deep into our bones, my body came to life when I heard the beat of the drum.

Some nights, as we fell into step beside each other, we'd drop bits of news about the goings-on in Egypt. When I first joined the dancing, I learned that long before I was born, Miriam's brother Moses had killed an Egyptian taskmaster and fled to Midian.

Years later, around the time I turned sixteen, the circle was once again abuzz with feverish whispers. Moses had returned, claiming that God had sent him to command Pharaoh to set us free. It didn't seem possible that we might go free after so many years in slavery. But then it didn't seem possible that we had held onto our rhythms and our melodies for seven generations either.

Every month, as we moved closer to the gathering of women, the drumming drowned out the chitchat. As our whispering melted into Miriam's beautiful melodies, the troubles of the world fell away.

In love You will lead us to freedom. In strength You will take us to Your holy land.

One night, as I danced past my grandmother, she pulled me toward her and placed the timbrel in my hands. She didn't have to say anything. My fingers already knew what to do.

I started tapping out a rhythm. Like magic, my grandmother rose from where she had been sitting, moving in time to the beat of my fingers.

When she danced, she didn't look old anymore. And when I played, I didn't feel like a slave anymore.

News of God's demands soon spread beyond our nighttime whispers. Pharaoh's refusal to heed Moses's words and let us go free brought on a series of terrifying plagues from God. The Nile River turned to blood. The land was infested with frogs and lice, wild beasts and locusts. The cattle fell ill. Our taskmasters were covered in boils. Hail pounded over the homes of our Egyptian neighbors, so loud that we could hear it in Goshen. But Pharaoh still refused to let us go. When he saw that the more severe plagues had spared the Hebrews, Pharaoh increased our workload to torment us.

Then a thick darkness fell over Egypt, as if we were walking through a storm cloud, even at midday. We couldn't get to our worksites, and our taskmasters could not pass through the darkness to find us. Another time, I might have relished the chance to rest. But sitting at home, not knowing what would happen next, was unbearable. I worried that the darkness would block out the approaching full moon. The idea of a month without dancing made my heart heavy.

When the darkness lifted, new rumors spread throughout Goshen: instructions from Moses to smear lamb's blood on our doorposts. This would protect us from the final plague, far more terrifying than those that had come before it. As the moon waxed full, Moses told us to stay home, pack light, and wait for his word to flee.

I grew restless, watching the full moon shine through our window. As midnight approached, my grandmother called me to her side.

"Our time in Egypt is coming to an end, Tehilah," she said. "Just as God promised our ancestors." She drew the timbrel from its hiding place in the wall. "Take this with you when we go."

"I can't take your timbrel!" I tried to refuse. "And anyway, Moses told us to pack only necessities."

"Our songs, our dances, these *are* necessities," she insisted. "They have kept us alive and hopeful all these years. And a miracle such as this will require a great celebration."

I trembled as she placed the timbrel in my hands. "Do you think there will really be a miracle?"

"I know it, in the depths of my heart," she replied. "That's why I've held onto this for so long. But it's your turn to lead the drumming now."

I held the drum against my heart as my grandmother put her arms around me. She held me close for a long time, until my father told us it was time to go.

By the light of the full moon, our people walked out of Egypt. The pounding of our feet on the hard sand sounded like a thousand drums. My heart thudded loudly in time with our steps, Miriam's melodies echoing in my mind.

God is my strength and my song.

I was flooded with questions. Where were we going? How would we survive along the way? Were we truly going to be free, after so many years of bitter slavery?

The thunder of horse hooves interrupted my thoughts. I didn't need to look behind me to know that Pharaoh had changed his mind and sent his army after us. The people in front of us stopped suddenly, and we slammed into them from behind. Looking up, we saw that the Sea of Reeds stretched out endlessly in front of us—a dead end.

"What does God want us to do now?" someone cried out. "Swim?" The people around me laughed bitterly. Few of us knew how to swim, and the waters before us looked choppy and rough.

Another called out to Moses, "Were there not enough graves in Egypt that you've brought us out here to die?"

"We were better off as slaves," someone shouted. "God is playing a cruel trick on us!"

But I said nothing, clutching the timbrel to my chest and humming Miriam's melody to myself.

God will be my deliverance.

I remembered my grandmother's words, the fire in her eyes when she handed me the timbrel. I felt her hand squeeze my shoulder. She believed with all her heart that there would be a miracle. And so did I.

In my old age, I would struggle to explain to my own grandchildren what it looked like when Moses lifted his staff and God parted the sea. No words could ever quite capture the smell of the salt air in my nostrils, the sting of sea spray on my cracked skin, the squish of fresh mud between my toes. Nor could words express what it felt like to walk between two towering walls of water and step safely onto dry land on the other side, heart pounding and breathless, as the parted sea came together again and the waves crashed over Pharaoh's army.

How could I describe being surrounded by so many people, standing silent and perfectly still? How could I tell them what it felt like to hold a thousand emotions in my heart at once: to be horrified at the sight of the Egyptians drowning and grateful that we had been spared? What could anyone say, or do, in that moment?

I hadn't realized how tightly I was holding the timbrel to my chest until I felt my arms stretch out in front of me. The rhythm pierced the silence as I tapped out a beat with my fingers. Soon I felt the breeze of countless bodies swaying in time with my drumming. Another beat rang out behind me, then another, as dozens of women fell into step beside me, clutching their own timbrels.

My grandmother wasn't the only one who had foreseen that we would need to celebrate this miracle with music. Soon we were moving in our familiar circles in this unfamiliar wilderness, weaving in and out of the crowds of men and boys.

A woman's voice called out over the drumming.

Who is like You, God, of all beings that are worshiped?

We raised our arms and our voices, repeating Miriam's verse.

The men stared at us in stunned silence, nearly as shocked to hear us all singing in unison as they'd been to see the waters part. But when Moses joined his sister in the singing, they raised their voices, too.

Who is like You, God, awesome in splendor, making miracles?

There would be countless miracles, large and small, in the years that followed: a sweet substance that fell from the sky to feed us when we were starving; wells of water that sprang up wherever Miriam set up camp; battles fought and won when we were hopelessly outnumbered. There would be difficult times as well, when we were frightened and frustrated, unsure of where we were going or when we would arrive.

No matter what happened, we were always singing. Our women still gathered by the light of the full moon, to remind ourselves of the songs and steps we'd learned in Egypt. But now that we were free, we could make music and dance in the daylight, loudly and without fear. Even long days of walking across the desert couldn't tire us. Like the generations before us, we sang songs of hope, adventure, and new beginnings.

And that felt like a miracle too.

CHAPTER ELEVEN

Standing, Sitting, and Signing at Sinai

WHEN MY FATHER TAUGHT ME THE STORY OF HOW THE world came to be, he said that every human being was created *b'tzelem Elohim*, in the image of God.

So I asked him, "Does God have wheels?"

My father looked confused. "Why would God have wheels?"

"You told me we were all created in the image of God," I replied, gesturing to my chair. "Doesn't that mean that God uses a wheelchair too?"

"Matan, sometimes you take things too literally." My father shook his head as he carefully considered his next words. "God is more enormous and more varied than anything we could imagine. But maybe some tiny part of God *does* use wheels. We each reflect only one tiny part of the whole."

It was a riddle I could never quite understand.

I've never been able to walk, because of something that happened to my legs before I was born. When I got too big to carry, my parents made me a wooden chair with metal wheels so that they could push me in front of them or pull me behind them. Sometimes, when we wanted to go really fast, we tied my chair to a donkey. But most of the time, once I was big enough, I pushed the wheels myself.

I didn't walk between walls of water when the Sea of Reeds parted; I rolled. I'd worried my wheels would get stuck in the muddy sea floor, but somehow I crossed just as quickly as the people who were walking and running. As I watched the wheels of Pharaoh's chariots sink uselessly into the mud, I realized that my chair's smooth passage had been part of God's miracle.

Even once we had crossed onto the dry land of the desert, I sometimes needed help getting around. My family, friends, and neighbors were quick to give it. I found plenty of ways to help them too. I could carry their kneading bowls in my lap when they got tired. Sometimes I rolled backward so that I could keep an eye on the stragglers and be on the lookout for robbers. When my friend Yiscah, who is blind, pushed my chair, I gave her directions and described the scenery we passed along the way. She told me that my detailed descriptions always made her smile. And when our friend Hanan, who is deaf, spoke in hand signs that Yiscah couldn't see, I made sure the two of them could understand each other.

It was a long journey, whether you could walk or not. But living in Egypt hadn't been easy either. Our taskmasters had always managed to find the hardest job that each of us could do. Surely God would be able to make good use of us in the wilderness, whether or not we could walk, or see, or hear.

Three months after we left Egypt, Moses came down from the mountain with a message from God.

"Prepare yourselves," he said. "In three days, all of us will stand before God at the foot of Mount Sinai to receive the Torah. Together, as one people, we will stand and see God's glory and hear God's Teaching."

Once again I was confused. Moses's words, too, felt like a riddle. How was I going to *stand* at Sinai? I'd never been able to stand in my entire life.

When I shared my question with my friends, they laughed.

"Matan, you take things too literally," said Yiscah. "We'll all *be* together, those of us who can stand and those of us who can't, those of us who can see and those who can't."

"Or maybe there will be a miracle," Hanan signed. "I'll be able to hear, Yiscah will be able to see, and you will be able to stand. Just for that moment. Or maybe from then on. Who knows?" He looked hopeful, though it was the first time I'd ever heard him say that he wished he could hear.

"If God wanted me to be able to stand or walk, or if God wanted Yiscah to be able to see and Hanan to be able to hear, wouldn't God have done that already? We were created in the image of God, right? Why would God change us, just so that we could all be standing at Sinai?"

"Yiscah and I could prop you up on our shoulders," Hanan suggested. "Then you could stand at Sinai, just like Moses said you would."

I was touched by Hanan's offer and Yiscah's eager nods of agreement. But my mind was made up. "If God doesn't want me there in my chair," I began, "how do I know that God wants me there at all?"

When the third day dawned, I stayed behind in my tent.

The summons to Sinai was impossible to ignore. If you couldn't see the bolts of lightning flash over the mountain, you could still hear the rumble of thunder and the blast of the shofar. If you couldn't hear, you could still smell the smoke coming out of the mountain. Even inside my tent, I could feel the heat rising from the endless stream of bodies winding their way toward Sinai.

My curiosity got the best of me. I lifted the flap of my tent and rolled outside to watch the procession. Sure enough, I could hear the faraway growl of thunder. Off in the distance, I could see plumes of smoke swirling over the distant mountain.

Maybe I had been too stubborn. Maybe my friends had been right and something miraculous would have happened if I'd joined my people at the mountain. Or my friends could have helped me, as they often did. I tried pushing myself up in my chair, to see if I was suddenly able to stand. But no, I just slid back into my seat. Even if I'd wanted to, I was now way too far behind the snaking tail of Israelites to catch up in my wheelchair.

"Have you finally decided to join us?" Yiscah's voice startled me. She and Hanan had been waiting next to the opening of my tent.

"You didn't think we'd go without you, did you?" Hanan signed. "What if I need an interpreter?"

"Or if I need a narrator?" Yiscah added, resting her hands on the back of my chair. "Or directions?"

"Seriously, though," Hanan signed, "every Israelite is meant to be at Sinai today. Whether you can stand or not. Maybe there will be a miracle. Maybe 'standing before God' is just a figure of speech. But whatever is going to happen when we get there, we all need to be there to find out!"

I shook my head. "It's probably too late."

"P-p-probably not," a familiar voice called from behind us. "They can't start without us."

"Moses?!" I exclaimed. I would have imagined that Moses would be the first person standing at the foot of Mount Sinai. But for some reason, he'd stayed behind, just like the three of us. I couldn't believe it. "Shouldn't you be at the mountain already?"

Moses raised an eyebrow. "I c-c-could ask you the same question." He signed as he spoke, so Hanan could follow.

My face flushed. "I can't stand at Sinai," I admitted, resting my hands in my lap. "I can't stand at all."

"And I c-c-can't say a full sentence without stuttering." Moses laughed. "But God still chose me to speak to Pharaoh. And to you."

"Isaac went blind," Yiscah added. "Leah had weak eyes, too. Jacob walked with a limp. God still chose them."

"You have your brother, Aaron, to help you speak," I said to Moses.

"What are we? Wet matzah?" Hanan signed. "Not to mention, sometimes we need your help too. I mean, have you ever met anyone who *never* needs help?"

Moses knelt in front of my chair, so that we would be face-to-face. "Do you know why I'm here, instead of being the first one standing at Sinai?"

I shook my head.

"Writing down God's Teaching is a lot of p-pressure," Moses said. "It has to be p-p-perfect."

I grimaced. "Not everything can be perfect."

"That's not what I meant." Moses paused and took a breath to slow his stutter. "Every letter is different, but not a single letter can be left out, or else it wouldn't say what God meant for it to say."

"What does that have to do with me?" I looked at my friends standing behind him. "With us?"

"God means for all of us to be at the foot of that mountain today," Moses said. "If even *one* of us is missing, it will be like the Teaching has a letter missing. It won't be saying what God meant for it to say." He gestured to Yiscah and Hanan. "And we're missing three of you."

"Four of us," I smiled at Moses.

Moses laughed. "Matan, you take things too literally."

"That's what people tell me," I said. "So…who's going to push my chair?"

Yiscah clapped her hands. "I'll do it!"

"Good! Now that that's settled"—Moses reached out his hands—"who's going to help the old man g-g-get up?"

Hanan pulled Moses to his feet, and the four of us moved toward the base of the mountain. As we came closer, the blast of the ram's horn grew louder. When I signed to Hanan that there was a shofar sounding, he signed back, "I can feel the vibrations."

Moses led us to a spot in the middle of the crowd. It was just large enough for the three of us, as if someone had saved it, knowing we were coming. Or as if we were the missing pieces of a puzzle, finally in place—pieces that together made up the image of God or the words of the Torah.

We watched as Moses waved and took off toward Mount Sinai.

Puffs of smoke swirled out of the mountain, gathering into a giant cloud. The cloud began to glow from within, as if it had swallowed the sun. I wished Yiscah could see it. But when I glanced behind me, she looked just as awestruck as the rest of us.

"It's so quiet," she whispered. "I can't even hear birds chirping!"

Sure enough, the usual hum of animal sounds had stopped. I might not have noticed the silence if Yiscah hadn't pointed it out.

While over a million Israelites stood in long rows at the foot of Mount Sinai, I sat in my chair. It didn't look like I would miraculously be able to stand to receive the Teaching. But it still felt like a small miracle that none of the tall people in front of me blocked my view.

The cloud above the mountain began to buzz with sounds I had never heard before. But somehow, with all of us present at the foot of the mountain, the sounds became words, and the words became God's Teaching.

"I am the Eternal your God who brought you out of the land of Egypt, from the house of bondage…"

On the way home, we argued over what we'd seen and what we'd heard, and how much of God's voice we had been able to handle before we begged Moses to step in and receive the Teaching on our behalf. Hanan told me he saw letters written in the smoke coming out of the mountain. Yiscah said she heard the words, but she also felt the letters under her fingertips. We debated what the Teaching sounded like and what parts of the Teaching were the most important. But all of us were there. And when God gave us the Torah, not a single letter was missing.

As it turns out, there *had* been a place for me at Sinai. Not just a place where I was welcome, but a place I needed to fill. I, Matan, needed to be there so that God's Teaching would be whole and complete. And people needed to see me there, as a person in a chair, so that everyone would know that the Torah was meant for me too. I'm glad my friends hadn't let me stay home.

Maybe sometimes I do take things too literally.

CHAPTER TWELVE

(Don't) Give Up Your Gold!

The night before I left Egypt, my neighbor Zahra decided to pierce my ears.

This wasn't out of character for Zahra, who spent her days following her architect father around his building sites when she should have been home learning to be a proper Egyptian lady; Zahra, who'd befriended me, a Hebrew, when most Egyptians treated us as if we were diseased.

Moses had sent us to borrow gold and silver from our Egyptian neighbors to take with us on our journey. But really, all I wanted was a chance to say goodbye.

I had barely knocked on the door when Zahra threw it open. "Pazi!" She threw her arms around me. "Are you really leaving Egypt?"

"Moses's prophecy has come true," I said. "We're going to be free."

Zahra pulled away, her eyes wet. "Come!" She pulled me inside the house. "Let me give you something to wear as a free woman!"

She unfastened the beautiful, gold hoop earrings she'd worn every day that I'd known her. I couldn't believe she was willing to part with them, much less give them to me.

"I can't take these," I insisted. "My ears aren't even pierced."

"I can fix that." Zahra smiled mischievously and brandished a sewing needle. "This way you'll never lose them."

I winced, anticipating the needle. "Are you sure?"

"Yes." Zahra ran the tip of the needle through the flame of her lantern. "Are you?"

I swallowed hard and took a deep breath. Then I nodded and closed my eyes.

In spite of the soreness, Zahra's earrings made me feel special. As we walked through the desert, bewildered by our newfound freedom, I'd raise my hands to my earlobes to make sure the hoops were still there, remembering Zahra's fierce look of concentration as she admired her handiwork.

My brother, Bahir, scoffed at Zahra's gift. "See if you can find somewhere to trade that junk for food."

But I treasured them nonetheless. They were the first things that were truly mine.

I wore them when we crossed the sea to freedom and when we stood at Sinai to hear the word of God. I was wearing them when Moses went up the mountain to receive God's Teaching.

Moses promised to return in forty days, but we quickly lost track of time. Waiting wasn't something we were used to. We might have spent four hundred *years* waiting to be free, but we hadn't spent any of those *days* waiting. We had been making bricks and hauling them up ramps from sunup to sundown, our skin cracking and peeling under the hot sun, trying to avoid the taskmasters' whips.

Even our early days in the wilderness were spent walking from place to place, setting up camp and taking it down again. But by the time Moses had left us to go up the mountain, our daily routine had become pretty, well... routine. Wake up. Eat manna. Wait. Sleep. Repeat. As the days wore on, we added "argue" to the list.

With so little to distract us, we should have done a better job counting. But the days started to run together. We were hot. Tired. Bored. Anxious. Confused. We started to pick fights with each other.

"He's *not* coming back," Bahir insisted. "It's been more than forty days."

"It hasn't!" I snapped back. "You've just lost count."

"So have you!" he yelled. And I couldn't really say anything, because he was right.

It seemed that every household in our camp was having the same fight. With every day that passed, our imaginations churned with worst-case scenarios. Murmurs began to spread through the camp that Moses had abandoned us or even that he'd died on the mountain. A group of people gathered at the foot of the mountain, where Aaron was stationed.

"Send someone up the mountain to see what happened to Moses," Bahir suggested.

"No one is allowed to touch the mountain," Aaron told us. "You could die."

"We could die out here without a leader," Bahir said.

"We can wait a little longer," Aaron insisted. "It hasn't been forty days yet. You've just lost count."

"*You've* lost count!" My brother's shouts attracted a crowd, and he fed on their energy, his voice growing louder and stronger as people clustered around him. "It's been weeks since we heard from Moses, or God," he cried. "We need a new leader to take us out of this place!"

The crowd behind him cheered in angry agreement. Aaron tried in vain to settle them down.

"We have a leader," Aaron said. "We have the most powerful God in the universe. Our God defeated Egypt with the plagues and cast Pharaoh's army into the sea."

"But where is God now?" Bahir shouted. "Where has God been all this time?"

"God is always with us," Aaron replied. "God cannot be seen or touched like the Egyptian gods. We have to have faith and trust each other. I promise you, Moses will be back!"

But the crowd at the foot of the mountain only grew larger and louder, demanding a god they could see and touch and follow, a god like the Egyptians had. As the hours passed, Aaron's shoulders sagged and his face fell. He looked exhausted, broken even, as people continued to scream in his face.

When he stood up straight again, there was a strange look on his face, as if he wasn't sure whether the idea he'd had was great, or terrible, or both.

"I will make a god for you, as you have asked," he shouted over the din. "Take off all your gold and bring it to me!"

Aaron enlisted a few young men with baskets to gather the gold, including Bahir. I was already looking for an escape route when he reached me, fixing his eyes on my gold hoops. "Pazi, hand them over."

I cupped my hands over my ears. "These were a gift from Zahra!"

"Zahra's people worked us to the bone," he snapped. "Let's put her gold to good use!"

"Don't you remember what we heard at Sinai?" I pleaded. "*You shall have no other gods beside Me…you shall not make sculptured images…you shall not bow down to them!*"

"God has abandoned us," Bahir said. "We need this gold to make something new."

I held my ground, and Bahir went on with his collecting. But I knew he'd be back. All around me, people were plucking off their jewelry. Family heirlooms, wedding presents, parting gifts from neighbors like Zahra—all of them tossed carelessly into the baskets. All because we were afraid. All because we were tired of waiting.

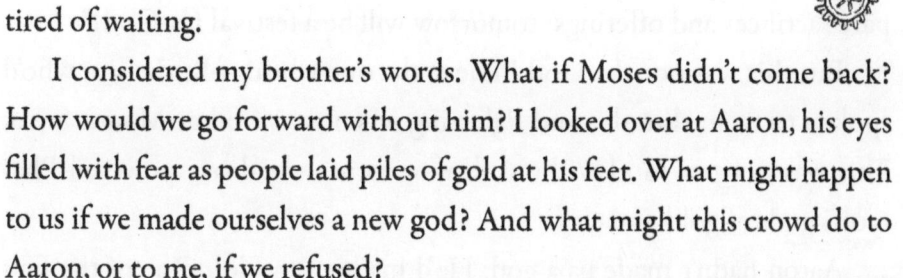

I considered my brother's words. What if Moses didn't come back? How would we go forward without him? I looked over at Aaron, his eyes filled with fear as people laid piles of gold at his feet. What might happen to us if we made ourselves a new god? And what might this crowd do to Aaron, or to me, if we refused?

I thought of Zahra, who wanted me to wear these earrings as a free person. This didn't feel like freedom. It felt like chaos. It felt wrong. I knew that Zahra would never have let anyone tell her what to do.

I caught the eyes of a few young women, still clutching their own earrings, bracelets, and necklaces, unwilling to part with them. Slowly, I stepped backward, motioning for the others to follow, trying not to call attention to myself. The others followed me, walking backward, until we could untangle ourselves from the crowd.

And then we ran.

We watched what happened next from a distance, huddled together on the edge of the camp, holding tightly to our necklaces and bracelets. Though we'd managed to hold on to what little gold we had, enough people had given theirs up to fill a big iron pot.

Aaron melted the gold into liquid and cast it into a mold. When the figure emerged from the fire, it looked just like the god-statue I'd seen in Zahra's house: a golden calf.

Aaron set the bull on a rock and built an altar beneath it. "This is your god, who brought you out of Egypt," he shouted to the crowd. "Prepare sacrifices and offerings; tomorrow will be a festival for God!"

But this was not the God I knew, the one who'd split the sea, who'd spoken to us in thunder and lightning when we stood at Mount Sinai. This was not our God without face or form, who'd overpowered Pharaoh's gods of gold and clay.

Aaron hadn't made us a god. He'd made... an idol. One of the first things God had told us not to make.

Either the people didn't notice or they didn't care. They greeted the gold god with the same fervor they'd shown when the sea split. They brought sheep, goats, and birds to make sacrifices. They ate too much meat and drank too much wine. They howled and beat their chests. They bowed before the calf and kissed its golden hooves.

As I watched the scene unfold, a young man joined us at the edge of the camp. I looked to see if he was protecting some precious gold item he'd saved from the fire. But his hands were open and empty. He told me his name was Bezalel.

"What are you doing here?" I asked. "Why aren't you worshiping the calf?"

"Honoring God is supposed to be something beautiful." Bezalel stared at the distant crowd. "They've turned it into something ugly."

Their frolicking was so frenzied and loud that only those of us looking on from the edge of camp saw Moses coming down the mountain, carrying two stone tablets engraved with God's Teaching. As he drew closer, I saw him freeze in horror at the wild scene below.

"What are you doing?" he bellowed at the crazed calf worshipers.

But either they didn't hear Moses or they didn't care. The people kept right on with their celebration.

"Stop that!" he shouted louder. "You're ruining everything!"

Bezalel and I watched as Moses tried to get everyone's attention. Finally, Moses raised the tablets high above his head. It was only after they came crashing to the ground that we realized what was happening.

The shattering stunned the revelers into silence. The singing and dancing stopped.

They looked up from the wine they were drinking, the meat they were eating, the feet they were kissing.

We'd broken God's covenant, and now God's Teaching was broken too.

For days following Moses's return, the camp was eerily silent, as quiet as it had been loud in the days before. Those who had been so eager to worship this new god watched in horror as Moses destroyed the calf, burning it to ash, grinding it to a powder. Shame weighed heavily on our shoulders, even for those of us who hadn't taken part in the revelry. Something sacred had been lost forever.

For a while, Moses disappeared again, and we didn't know if he, or God, would lead us any farther. If we had thought waiting was tough before, it was excruciating now. Would God forgive us? Was there any hope left of us reaching the Promised Land now?

While we waited, Bezalel and I and a few others walked around the base of the mountain, searching for pieces of the broken tablets. Maybe we could put them back together. I spotted a chunk of stone with an *alef* on it. But when I knelt to pick it up, it crumbled at my touch.

Still, some things could be rebuilt, and our covenant with God was one of them.

When Moses appeared before us again, his face was pale and his head was bowed, but he didn't look angry anymore. Once more, he carried two stone tablets with him. But these tablets were blank.

"I'm going up the mountain again," he told us. "God is giving us another chance."

"So what do we do now?" I asked.

"We try again," Moses said, "and pray that we do better this time."

Moses told us he'd be gone for forty days. This time we kept count. Aaron would still be in charge, but this time we had something important to fill our days.

"Everyone who has gifts to give, bring them to Bezalel," Moses had directed us before he left, putting his hand on Bezalel's shoulder. "Everyone who is wise in heart, come help him build a place to honor God."

Bezalel stepped forward and showed us the designs that God had given Moses: a huge tent made of animal skins and embroidered tapestries; wood planks, a stone altar, and fixtures made of gold.

A groan went up from the crowd. So much gold had gone into making the calf. How could we possibly have enough left?

Bezalel seemed to read our minds. "The past is in the past," he said. "We made a mistake, and we've been given a second chance. Now *this* will be the place where God will dwell. *This* is where we'll bring our offerings and listen to God's Teaching. It will come with us wherever we go. And God will too."

I looked at the other young women who had held onto their jewelry and found them looking back at me, waiting to see what I would do.

I didn't hesitate. I walked up to Bezalel and handed him my earrings.

He looked at me with caution. "Are you sure?"

I swallowed hard and took a deep breath. Then I nodded and closed my eyes.

The others followed close behind, depositing their jewelry into Bezalel's open palms.

"I know how special these are to you," Bezalel said. "With this gold, we'll make a place to keep God's Teaching. So that it can't be broken again."

Bezalel asked Aaron to help him melt down our gold. Meanwhile, carpenters sanded acacia wood into planks for an Ark to hold the new set of tablets. The Ark would be coated with gold—our gold—inside and out, to protect what was most precious to us.

"Come with me," I said, gesturing to my friends. "I have an idea."

While Bezalel put the finishing touches on the Ark, we walked around the base of the mountain again, carefully picking up the pieces of the first set of tablets. We brought them to Bezalel, who placed them inside the Ark. They were beautiful and broken—just like us. We wouldn't forget what we'd done, how scared we'd been, the mistakes we'd made. We'd carry all of that with us, as we went forward and tried to do better this time.

When Moses returned, he laid the newly carved tablets in the Ark next to the old ones, carefully, as if he were laying a baby to sleep in a basket. He smiled when Bezalel showed him the broken pieces already in the Ark. It was the first smile we'd seen from him in a long time.

When we were ready to march forward again, a glint of sunlight caught on one of the gold rings of the Ark. I'd never know exactly where Zahra's gold earrings had been used. But I knew that her gift had found its proper place.

CHAPTER THIRTEEN

Follow That Goat!

In the weeks leading up to the sacred ritual, our parents started using a new word. They spoke it only in hushed tones, which gave it the magic of something dangerous and forbidden.

Azazel.

My sister Yael and I weren't sure what it meant—or even whether it was a person, place, or thing. We knew it had something to do with Aaron the high priest, a pair of goats, and being forgiven for our mistakes one day each year. But everything else about it was shrouded in mystery.

Azazel.

My friends and I used it as a swear word or a magical incantation. I told Yael that if she said *Azazel* three times, a demon would appear and steal her away into the wilderness.

"Aren't we already in the wilderness?" Yael looked at me sideways, like she knew I was making things up but wasn't quite sure.

"Compared to where this demon would take you," I said, shaking my head solemnly, "this wilderness would look like the Garden of Eden."

After that, Yael stopped putting the lamp out before she went to sleep. I knew I'd gotten under her skin. Scaring her with tales of *Azazel* became my new favorite pastime.

I blamed *Azazel* for snapped tent poles and burnt soup, anything that broke or spilled. If Yael tripped and fell, I told her that *Azazel* must have gotten her. I teased her until she ran away, shrieking with terror.

Our parents were not amused. "Don't joke about things you don't understand, Tzvi," they scolded, looking a little nervous. "You don't even know what…*that word*…means."

"Fine," I countered. "Tell me what it means!"

They looked at each other blankly. Like me, they knew it had something to do with the sacred ritual, but that was about it.

Adults were supposed to fast for the entire day of the sacred ritual, starting at sundown the night before. To prepare for the pre-fast meal, Yael had milked our goats into a large clay jug that she'd made herself. She'd spent the last few days painting two goats on it, a nod to the mysterious ritual whose name she could not say without trembling.

In the early afternoon, Yael went off with our parents to wash up and dress for the holiday. I stayed behind, not wanting to spend the rest of the day trying not to get dirty. When the three of them were gone, I grabbed the sheepskin ball I'd made and took it outside to practice kicking, using the opening of our tent as a goalpost.

Suddenly, I heard a loud *crash* and looked down to find a river of white liquid pooling at my feet, with a shard of clay floating in it. I recognized the tail of one of the goats Yael had painted. *The milk jug!*

I looked to my left and then to my right, to see if anyone had seen me. Then I stashed the ball behind our tent and ran off to wash off my feet.

Everyone was in a bad mood at dinner, which didn't bode well for how we might feel *after* a day of fasting. Yael looked heartbroken that her hard work had gone to waste.

"I was so *careful* putting the jug down," she kept saying, shaking her head. "How could it break into so many pieces just from falling over?" She glared at me, as if she knew I was hiding something. Which I was.

The words were out of my mouth before I could stop them: "Maybe it was *Azazel*."

Yael's eyes widened. Her voice dropped to a shaky whisper. "It couldn't be." She looked to our parents for reassurance. "Could it?"

"I don't know where you came up with this nonsense," our father said, glaring at me. "But whoever, or whatever, *Azazel* is, I doubt it spends its days terrorizing children and knocking over milk jugs." He turned to Yael. "I'm sure it was just an accident. Right, Tzvi?"

I mumbled in agreement. But Yael wasn't convinced. She left her food untouched and didn't say another word for the rest of the night.

The next morning, we all walked together to the Tent of Meeting for the sacred ritual. Our parents were already short-tempered from hunger, and Yael seemed nervous and jumpy. It was hot and crowded by the entrance to the Tent of Meeting, where Aaron, the high priest, stood in his plain linen garments. Two assistants stood beside him, and in front of them, a pair of goats, bleating and squirming like they didn't know what was about to happen—or maybe like they did.

"Today is the Day of Atonement," Aaron pronounced. "Today, we ask the Eternal our God to forgive the mistakes we've made this past year." He gestured to the two goats. "We will sacrifice one of these goats on the altar in atonement for all of our wrongdoing."

"What's atonement?" Yael whispered.

"It's like an apology," our mother whispered back, "one we make to God."

Aaron went on, "We will send the other goat into the wilderness alive, carrying away all of our people's misdeeds, marked for *Azazel*."

Something about hearing the word come out of the high priest's mouth made my hair stand on end. I turned to Yael, whose face was pale and a little green. Her hands were shaking too. I couldn't tell whether it was hearing the forbidden word spoken aloud or the thought of one of the goats being sacrificed. Or both.

"Now we will draw lots to choose which goat is for the Eternal," Aaron continued, "and which is for *Azazel*." His assistants held out a wooden box. Aaron closed his eyes and put both hands in at once, pulling out two slips of paper and handing them to his assistants to read.

The assistant on Aaron's right called out, "For the Eternal!" A cheer rose up from the crowd as the goat on Aaron's right was taken inside to be sacrificed. Apparently, it was a good omen when the lot for the Eternal came from Aaron's right hand. It didn't feel like such a good omen for the goat though.

A cloud of smoke wafted out of the Tent of Meeting. Someone was burning incense, probably to cover the stench of the soon-to-be-slaughtered goat. The left goat sneezed. It was such a funny sound that a giggle escaped from my throat before I could stop it. But almost as quickly, I started to feel bad for laughing at the poor creature.

Yael said aloud what I was thinking: "What happens to the other goat?"

We waited until Aaron returned from inside the Tent of Meeting and laid his hands on the goat designated for *Azazel*. "Eternal our God," he prayed, "the people of Israel have missed the mark before You. We have disobeyed, we have lied, we have hurt our loved ones. We have spent these past few weeks making amends and asking forgiveness from one another. Now, on this Day of Atonement, we humbly ask You to forgive us. As we send this goat out into the wilderness, may it carry all of our heartbreak away."

Instinctively, my hands flew to my own heart. Yael had been so sad and scared the whole day, and all because of me and my stupid lie. It wasn't just the milk jug I'd broken. I'd broken her trust.

The goat sneezed again. How could such a small creature carry away all of our mistakes? And how could it carry away the hurt I'd caused Yael when I hadn't even bothered to ask her for forgiveness?

"Yaeli," I whispered, "I need to tell you something."

Yael kept staring straight ahead, her arms folded over her chest. Aaron called to the man who would lead the goat into the wilderness, handing him the end of the rope that was tied around the creature's neck.

I nudged Yael, but she kept right on ignoring me. The man started to lead the goat away from the Tent of Meeting. If the goat went to *Azazel*—whatever that meant—before I could apologize, I'd be stuck carrying this bad feeling around for another year, until the next Day of Atonement.

"Yaeli!" I whispered again.

This time she turned to me and hissed, "What?!"

I wanted to confess, to apologize, but the words were caught in my throat. So instead, I asked her, "Want to go see what happens to the goat?"

We wove our way out of the crowd in front of the Tent of Meeting, trying to keep pace with the man and the goat, without getting too close to them. We followed the man as he led the goat through the mostly empty camp and into the craggy terrain beyond the camp's furthermost border. The dry land was studded with sharp rocks and pointy brambles. I glanced behind me, but we were already so far from the camp that I couldn't see it anymore.

When I turned back toward the man, I found that he, too, had turned around and was now standing right in front of us.

"What are you doing here?" he growled.

From a distance, I hadn't realized how big and rough-looking he was. Of course he would have to be, for Aaron to choose him to deliver a goat to a demon. Or whatever.

I toyed with the idea of telling a lie and seeing how much more trouble I could get myself into on the holiest day of the year.

But Yael spoke first: "We wanted to see what happens to the goat." She seemed surprised by her own boldness and immediately cast her eyes down at the ground. The man looked to me for further explanation. I decided, for once, to tell the truth.

"I didn't get a chance to apologize to my sister," I blurted. Even though this man was a stranger, I poured out the whole story about the jug, the ball, and the lie, and how I'd kept scaring Yael with the threat of a demon stealing her away.

From the corner of my eye, I could see Yael's face glowing red with anger.

But the man listened patiently, gently petting the goat with his rough hands. When I finished, he murmured with understanding. "You didn't want the goat to go off to *Azazel* before you'd made things right with your sister?"

I nodded.

"So…" The man gestured to Yael. "Make things right with your sister." He stared at me as I stood with my mouth hanging open. "I'll wait."

I took a deep breath. Yael's face was still clouded with anger. "Yaeli, I'm sorry I broke the milk jug. I'm even more sorry that I lied about it. I should have told you the truth, instead of blaming it on *Azazel* and scaring you."

"I wasn't scared," Yael insisted. "But you're right. You should have told me the truth."

The man chuckled. "You really blamed it on *Azazel*?"

Suddenly it dawned on me that we had a chance to have our question answered, once and for all. "What is *Azazel*, anyway?"

"Or who?" Yael added. "Or where?"

The man swept his hands across the rocky wasteland. "This place we're standing in?" he said. "This wilderness is *Azazel*. The high priest sent me here to release the goat. But first…" He held out his arm. There was a length of red string wrapped around his wrist, which he unwound and snapped into two pieces. "Tie this piece around one of the goat's horns." He handed one piece to me. "Hold onto this one." He handed the other half to Yael.

"What's this for?" Yael asked.

"When the people of Israel are forgiven, the string will turn white," he answered.

"Like washing out a stain?" Yael suggested.

"Kind of," the man answered. "That's why we keep a piece with us, so we'll know when the change happens." He gave Yael a moment to pet the goat one last time, then loosened the rope from around its neck and gave it a gentle shove. It scampered away across the uneven ground.

The man sat down on one edge of a wide rock, patting the space beside him. "Now we wait."

We sat there in silence for a long time, watching the goat trot away. A few times, it ambled back to us, and the man gave it another shove. Eventually it got the hint.

The goat went farther. Sometimes it stumbled over an unseen rock or got tangled up in the brambles.

Yael stood up from the rock, her face full of worry. "Shouldn't we help it?"

The man gently put his hand on Yael's shoulder and eased her back down. "It'll figure it out," he said. "It's just wandering."

"Like us?" I mused.

"Like us," the man nodded. "Much of the time it doesn't know where it is or where it's going. Sometimes it stumbles, sometimes it falls, but it gets back up again. That's life. Sometimes we get stuck. But we can get unstuck too."

I looked at the goat. Sure enough, it shook itself free, trotted over to a shrub, and munched on some leaves. As the day wore on, it wandered farther and farther away, until finally we couldn't see it anymore.

"Yaeli," I said. "I really am sorry. I won't lie to you again."

"I know." Yael patted my hand. "I forgive you." She glanced down at the piece of string she was holding, which had faded from red to white. The people had been forgiven too. "Is it really that simple?" Yael asked the man.

"Not always," he sighed. "But as far as today is concerned, yes, it is." He stood up and offered us his hands. Together we walked back to camp, taking care not to stumble over the jagged rocks, taking care not to let each other fall.

CHAPTER FOURTEEN

Please, God, Heal Her

Being the high priest was not as glamorous as Aaron had expected. It could actually be pretty messy.

The fancy outfit had nearly fooled him. But mere moments after he donned the fine linen tunic and colorful embroidered apron, his brother Moses had poured oil over Aaron's head, slaughtered a bull in front of him, and smeared its blood on his ear, thumb, and big toe. Aaron knew this was a part of the ceremony that made him high priest, but Moses seemed to enjoy it a little too much.

Aaron worried about getting his new clothes dirty. Bezalel and his crew had spent weeks decorating them with embroidered pomegranates and golden bells. They were beautiful. Why did Aaron have to dress that way to work almost entirely with blood and fire? It was a mystery to him.

Moses got to speak directly with God. Miriam was in charge of finding water and leading the people in song and dance. Moses told Aaron he'd be working in the Tent of Meeting, where the Israelites gathered to get close to God. But "getting close" mostly meant sacrificing animals: slicing them open, draining their blood, burning the fatty parts on the altar, "to make a pleasing odor for God," Moses told him.

Aaron did not find the odor pleasing. He spent most days holding his breath and trying not to throw up. Just as he was getting used to it, Moses revealed the *worst* part of the high priest's job: examining the Israelites for *tzara'at*.

Tzara'at could look like a rash or a burn, a hairy patch on the skin or a bald spot on the head, red-streaked swelling or flaky white scales. It could seep into clothing or spread through the walls of a house. And it was Aaron's job, along with the other priests, to diagnose it.

"Why do the priests have to deal with all these sick people?" Aaron asked.

"Because you are in charge of sacred objects and sacred gatherings," Moses explained. "And people who have *tzara'at* can't come near either of those things." Moses went on to tell him how anyone with symptoms of *tzara'at* needed to be isolated for seven days, then checked again to see if the infection had spread. "Make sure they stay away from everyone else until it's gone."

The isolation turned out to be the hardest thing about having *tzara'at*, even worse than the symptoms. If a rash or a burn turned out to be *tzara'at*, people who were infected had to tear their clothes, uncover their heads, and cover their mouths. When they walked through the camp, they were instructed to shout, "Impure! Impure!" so that everyone else knew to stay away.

It was humiliating. Aaron hated seeing the look on people's faces when he gave them these instructions.

No one knew exactly how people got *tzara'at* or why. Rumors began to spread that it was a divine punishment for something. Everyone had theories as to the cause: gossip, lying, even murder. Still, no one could say for sure. Not even Aaron.

The theory that *tzara'at* was a punishment from God made it easier for people to believe that it wouldn't happen to them so long as they behaved themselves. It made it easier for Aaron too. He spent so much time with people in pain, people who were lonely and isolated. It was easier to bear if he could imagine that they'd brought it on themselves somehow.

"You have to be more careful," Aaron told one young man, as he examined a suspicious patch of yellow hair on his arm.

"Careful about *what*?" the man asked. "I don't even know how I got it!"

"You must have done *something* wrong," Aaron insisted. Often, when Aaron said this, the patients would confess something they'd done, eyes cast down, face red with shame.

But this young man just scratched his head. Aaron couldn't tell if he was deep in thought or just itchy. When he spoke, his voice cracked. "I try so hard to be good."

"Try harder," Aaron said, as he explained the isolation instructions. "This will fade away soon enough, but you don't want to get it again."

"But I still don't know how I got it!" Tears of frustration flowed freely down the young man's face. "Some help *you* are!"

Soon Aaron stopped saying anything aside from God's instructions. There wasn't much he could do for them, anyway. There wasn't any definite explanation for *tzara'at*, and there wasn't any cure. After a while, Aaron didn't even look at the people's faces as he diagnosed their rashes and burns. He simply recited the rules and told them when to come back for another examination, all with his eyes on the ground.

When he finished, he'd send them on their way, grateful that nothing like this could ever happen to him or his family.

Or so he thought.

Aaron had never understood why his sister and sister-in-law didn't get along. But Miriam and Tzipporah were always stepping on each other's toes. They were both so protective of Moses, so eager for his attention, that they got in each other's way. And Moses, who increasingly gave his attention only to God, barely seemed to notice either of them.

One day Aaron came out of the Tent of Meeting to find the two of them arguing.

"Stop sticking your nose in other people's business!" Tzipporah said sharply.

"It's my business too," Miriam cried. "He's my brother. Pharaoh would have killed him in his cradle if not for me."

"He's *my* husband. And he would have died in Midian if not for me," Tzipporah snapped. "I can take care of this myself."

Miriam was furious. She called Tzipporah a name—an ugly one. Aaron had never heard her use such language before in her life. His face flushed as Tzipporah turned on her heel and stormed away.

"That woman is impossible!" Miriam groaned to Aaron. "I was only trying to help." Aaron started to ask her what had happened—he had no idea what they'd been fighting about—but Miriam kept talking, her eyes full of tears. "Moses is the same way. He has to do everything himself. Does he think God talks only to him? You and I are prophets, too!"

Aaron's first thought was, *Don't drag me into this*. But his sister had a point. "Why does Moses get to make all the decisions?" Aaron hadn't realized he was angry until the words tumbled out of his mouth. "While I'm stuck looking at rashes and cleaning up animal entrails? What makes *him* so special?"

Aaron noticed that Miriam's face had gone pale while he was speaking. He turned to find their brother standing behind him, looking hurt.

"Is that really how you feel?" Moses asked quietly.

Aaron opened his mouth to explain. But before he could speak, a thick cloud fell over the three of them, accompanied by a loud crack of thunder. Then, just as quickly, it was gone.

And Miriam was screaming.

Aaron turned to find his sister covered in white scales. Even without coming closer, Aaron could tell they were *tzara'at*. He wondered if the rumors were true: that *tzara'at* was a punishment for gossiping. Maybe it was just a terrible coincidence.

Aaron looked down at his own hands, but the skin was as smooth as it had always been. If this was a punishment for what Miriam had said, Aaron had been just as much in the wrong. It didn't seem fair. He hated seeing Miriam in so much pain. But even worse than the scales on her skin was the look of shame in her eyes.

"I'll have to leave the camp," Miriam whispered. "Everyone will know what I've done."

Aaron grasped Moses's hands. "Moses!" he pleaded. "Don't make her suffer like this. It was my fault. Tell God to punish me instead."

Moses shook his head. "You know I can't do that."

"You have to do *something*!" Aaron exclaimed. "Have some compassion!"

"Compassion?" Moses looked Aaron right in the eyes. "Aren't you the one who keeps telling people it's their own fault when they get sick?"

Aaron cringed. Moses was right. Miriam was his sister, so he didn't want her to suffer. But all of those people he'd sent away hurting and ashamed? They were part of somebody's family too.

"Please?" Aaron begged.

Moses looked at Miriam, who was crying softly, her head bowed low to the ground. He lifted his face to the sky and prayed. "*El na r'fa na lah! Please, God, please, heal her!*"

Aaron looked at his sister, waiting for a sudden transformation. There was none. Miriam's skin was still white as snow. Her sobs grew louder as she turned toward the outer edge of the camp, where people with *tzara'at* dwelled in tents by themselves until they recovered.

Aaron hated hearing her cry. He could tell that his brother did too. She'd always taken such good care of both of them.

"We won't go anywhere until you're better," Moses promised. "The whole camp will wait for you to heal."

But Miriam only cried harder. "I'll be all alone out there."

"No, you won't," Aaron promised. "I'll go with you."

Aaron walked to the edge of the camp with his sister. He couldn't go into the tent with her, but for seven days, he sat outside in a plain linen tunic. He brought her food and water and anything else she asked for. And when there was nothing he could bring her, nothing else he could do to help, he'd lean in close to the opening of the tent and tell her stories, make jokes, anything to let her know she wasn't alone.

In the Tent of Meeting, he had so much power. But here, all he could do was sit near her.

One day Tzipporah came by with a satchel slung over her arm. "Herbal remedies from my people," she said, as she laid out her supplies on the ground outside the tent.

"There's no cure for this," Aaron tried to tell her.

Tzipporah nodded in understanding. "This will help her feel better until it goes away."

Miriam must have heard them talking from inside the tent. "Tzipporah?" she called softly, then burst into tears again. "I'm so sorry I said all those horrible things. I shouldn't have meddled in your business."

Tzipporah leaned against the tent flap. "That's all over now. Let's see if we can make you feel better." Tzipporah handed Miriam a compress through the opening of the tent. "All the Israelites are waiting for you and praying for your recovery."

This, more than anything, seemed to lift Miriam's spirits. Her crying quieted, and she drifted off to sleep. As Miriam rested, Aaron looked around at all the other tents lined up along the edge of the camp. Each of them, he had come to realize, held a person just like his sister, someone who was suffering and in pain. What they needed, more than any diagnosis or treatment, was to know that they weren't alone.

Aaron gestured to Tzipporah's satchel. "Maybe we can help the others too?"

Together they moved from tent to tent, bringing food and water and soothing herbs to the other people in isolation. Sometimes Aaron would ask the people how they were feeling and listen as they told their story. Sometimes he'd just sit outside their tents in silence. And when he heard someone crying, he'd lean against the opening of the tent and whisper, "You're not alone. You won't feel this way forever. And we're not going anywhere without you."

His words were all he had to give. He hoped that they would be enough.

CHAPTER FIFTEEN

Seeing through Caleb Eyes

It was nice to have a friend who always looked on the bright side. Caleb was that kind of friend.

Back when we'd first left Egypt, walking between walls of water that had once been the Sea of Reeds, most Israelites had looked down at the seabed, complaining about the muck squishing against their sandals. Only Caleb looked up at the horizon.

"Joshua! We're free!" he shouted. "It's a miracle!" (Caleb used a lot of exclamation points.)

He'd said the same thing when we stood at Sinai, and when Moses came down from the mountain with the second set of tablets, and when Bezalel showed us the Ark of the Covenant. Even on more ordinary days, when all we did was trudge through the desert, Caleb would suddenly look up and exclaim, "Joshua! We're free!"

If I didn't respond, Caleb would elbow me in the ribs to make me pay attention. No matter what troubles were on my mind, I'd look up at the wilderness stretched out before us and allow myself to feel hopeful, just for a moment.

"A miracle!" I'd concede, rubbing my side.

As our days of wandering stretched into months, Caleb's optimism began to get on people's nerves, including mine. Life in Egypt had been hard, but so far life as a free people hadn't been much easier.

In Egypt, everything had been decided for us: where to go, what to do, where our next meal was coming from. Now nothing was certain. Every day there was another setback. And even when there wasn't, we found plenty to complain about.

The flaky, sweet manna that appeared like fresh dew each morning was too bland. The water that sprung up miraculously in the desert was too bitter. Even God's voice at Sinai was too piercing for our fragile human ears.

Caleb kept trying to boost the people's spirits. After a few weeks, some of our fellow wanderers coined the term "Caleb eyes" to refer to his rose-colored way of seeing things. It wasn't a compliment. It was usually accompanied by an eye roll.

"Aren't you even a *little* excited?" Caleb asked the others on our tribal council. "We're headed to the Promised Land!"

"Why should we be excited?" groaned Sethur. "How do we know we won't end up starving, or slaves again, or both?"

"If we even manage to *get* to the Promised Land," mumbled Palti.

"Who's to say we'll be able to conquer it?" Gaddiel asked. "We're no army. We're just a bunch of tired slaves."

While Caleb reassured us that better days were coming, I worried that the grumblers were right. How could we know what awaited us on the other side of the Jordan River? The suspense might kill us—if the wilderness didn't kill us first.

So when Moses asked me to lead a group of twelve scouts to inspect the Promised Land, I quickly agreed. I wanted to see if the Promised Land was, well, as promised.

"I'm counting on you to get the whole story," Moses told me. "Even with God's help, we're going to have many challenges to face when we arrive in the Promised Land. We need to know what we're up against."

Caleb could hardly contain himself when I invited him to come along. He practically bounced behind me, chattering on about everything we passed along the way. I could tell that the other scouts were working hard not to tell Caleb to shut up.

Soon we found ourselves in another desert, not unlike the one we'd left behind: dry and cracked from the late-summer heat. There wasn't a person—or a plant—anywhere in sight.

"Nice milk and honey," muttered Nahbi.

"At least there aren't any people here," said Geuel. "I guess we can see why."

"Now wait a minute," I countered. "Don't give up on it yet." Caleb nodded in agreement.

As we walked further north, I noticed that the cities we passed were surrounded by high stone walls. They wouldn't be easy to breach in a battle, if it came to that. We had our work cut out for us. Was this dry, dusty desert even worth it?

Suddenly the dry, brown land exploded into every shade of green. The hill country was studded with lush, leafy trees, their branches practically pulled to the ground by the weight of their fruit.

"Look at this!" Caleb grabbed a pomegranate that was roughly the size of my head. "Have you ever seen fruit this big?"

Sethur folded his arms across his chest. "It's probably poisonous."

"Let's take it back to show Moses," I suggested.

But Caleb wasn't listening. He split the fruit open and scooped a handful of seeds into his mouth. "This," he declared as the juice dribbled down his chin, "is the best pomegranate I've ever tasted." He hacked the fruit into twelve pieces with his knife. "Here, try some!"

"Yeah," scoffed Gaddi. "Because nothing bad ever happened from someone saying, 'Here, eat this fruit.'"

"Enough!" Sick of their grumbling, I grabbed the fruit from Caleb, slurping the red seeds until juice ran down my forearms. The others hesitated at first, but thirst and curiosity got the best of them. We feasted on the fruit, playfully spitting seeds at each other. It had been a while since we had tasted anything so tart—manna was, in fact, bland and sickly sweet too. Soon we were giddily pointing out the different fruits growing all around us. For a moment, I let myself stop worrying.

"Look at these grapes!" Yigal cut a heavy bunch from a drooping vine. "It would take two of us to carry them." He draped them over his walking stick and handed the other end to Palti.

Even Sethur started to waver. "I wonder if there are any oranges. I haven't had an orange since..."

BOOM! The ground beneath us shook.

"Earthquake?" Gaddi warned. But the shaking didn't stop. It felt as if it was steadily moving closer to us. The pounding sound grew louder. A shadow fell over us.

"That's not an earthquake," I whispered. "It's..."

"A giant!" screamed Sethur. "RUN!!!"

For that moment, we were all in agreement. We ran as fast as we could out of the hill country, never daring to look behind us. When we were finally safely back in the desert, we collapsed onto the dry ground, gasping for breath.

For a long time, nobody said anything. I was going to have to break the silence, but I wasn't sure what to say. Moses trusted us to bring back a truthful report. But what was the truth?

I took a deep breath. "Before we go back across the river," I said, "we need to get our story straight. We need to give one, honest report to Moses and the people, so they'll know what to expect when we enter the land."

"What's to get straight?" Shammua said. "We can't bring the people back there. We were nearly attacked by a giant!"

"Giants, plural," said Yigal. "There was definitely more than one."

"We didn't even see them!" Caleb protested. "How do you know they were giants?"

"Didn't you feel the ground shaking?" asked Ammiel. "Or see how their shadows blocked the sun?"

"It could have been an earthquake," Caleb suggested. "Or an eclipse?"

Even I rolled my eyes at this theory. Yes, some of the scouts were stretching the truth. But that didn't mean there wasn't any danger lurking in the land. Did Caleb not see that? Or was he choosing to ignore it?

Sethur interrupted my thoughts with a loud snort. "Are you saying we *didn't* just get run out of the hill country by someone—or some*thing*—trying to attack us?"

"I'm *not* saying that," said Caleb. "But that doesn't mean it was an army of sun-blocking, earth-shaking giants!"

"No," muttered Ammiel. "It was clearly an earthquake-eclipse combo. Those happen *all* the time."

The conversation devolved even further from there. The story of the giant, or giants, became more and more wild and elaborate. There were five giants, ten giants, fifty. They were as tall as oak trees; solid and impenetrable like stone towers. One giant was so big that he looked like he was wearing the sun as a necklace.

My head started pounding. None of us had seen the source of the sound, or the shaking, or the shadow. We'd run away too fast, and now our imaginations were running away from us. Moses was relying on us to tell the truth. But the lies kept growing louder. Caleb's hopeful chatter grew louder too. Soon it all began to sound like ringing and buzzing in my ears.

"Wait a minute," Caleb said. "Not everything was bad. Remember the green hills? The giant fruit?"

"And the giant people," said Nahbi. "They made us look like grasshoppers. They could crush us under their feet and not even feel it."

"The Israelites are going to be crushed when we tell them," said Shaphat.

"We had one close call with one bigger-than-average guy. We can't give up yet." Caleb looked at me pleadingly. "Joshua, say something!"

"What do you want me to say, Caleb?" I shouted. "That there's nothing to be afraid of? That everything's a miracle and we can just waltz in tomorrow and build a nation, no problem? Who cares how big the grapes are? Who cares if it was a giant or an earthquake or an eclipse? *Something* chased us out of the land. If we look at it only with your Caleb eyes, we're going to get everyone killed!"

Caleb looked as if I'd slapped him. I struggled to find words that might make things better. But before I could say anything else, I heard a loud cry rise up behind me. While I'd been yelling at Caleb, we'd crossed into the Israelite camp, where the people were waiting eagerly for our report. It seems I had unwittingly given it to them.

It wasn't clear how much the waiting crowd had heard, but it didn't matter. Soon the people had gathered at Moses's tent, demanding to go back to Egypt.

"Back to Egypt?!" Moses cried. "What could possibly make you want to go *back to Egypt*?"

The people relayed the rumors that had been tearing through the camp. *The Promised land is full of giants. And armies. And armies of giants. Walled cities and poisonous pomegranates.*

"That one's not even a little bit true," muttered Caleb. "Sethur made that up!"

But the more ridiculous the rumors became, the harder they were to ignore. Finally Moses blew a shofar, silencing the crowd. "Scouts, tell us the truth. What did you see?"

Shammua spoke first: "The land *is* just as God promised: lush, green, flowing with milk and honey…" From the first word that he spoke, though, the Israelites only heard the "but…" that was coming.

It came from Sethur. "*But*…it is also filled with powerful armies and fortified cities…"

"And giants," added Nahbi. "We looked like grasshoppers."

Moses turned to me. "Joshua, is this true?"

I felt my tongue stick to the roof of my mouth. The scouts' report was only a partial truth, and the worst possible version of it. The people needed to hear Caleb's perspective too. And mine, whatever that might be. But there were now ten scouts, plus thousands of Israelites, clamoring to go back to Egypt. If I sided with Caleb, it would be the two of us against everyone.

While I was trying to decide what to do, Caleb called out in a clear, loud voice, "This is nonsense!" The crowd hushed for a moment. "Sure, there are obstacles to overcome. But God promised us this land. Whatever challenges await us there, we can face them together! Let's go up and conquer this land!"

But the damage had already been done. A shadow had fallen over the Israelites' faces, darker even than the one the alleged giant had cast.

"Of course Caleb would see only the good!" said Sethur. "He's going to get us killed!"

"Take us back to Egypt!" Ammiel shouted. "We don't want to die out here!"

"It's better to live as slaves than die by the sword!" said Gaddi. "We have to protect our families!"

The people burst out wailing, so loudly that it sounded as if even the animals had joined in.

"Joshua?" Moses pleaded. "Who's telling the truth? What did you really see?"

I wanted to see things the way that Caleb did. I wanted to get to the Promised Land and build a nation there with my people. But the people had made up their minds. Anything Moses or Caleb said to reassure them only made them angrier. Some of them had even picked up stones to throw at our heads.

"I...uh..." I looked at Caleb, but he turned away from me and walked out of the camp. "I need to go talk to Caleb," I said and ran after him.

I found Caleb sitting on a rock, throwing pebbles into the Jordan River. He didn't move when I sat down beside him. "What happened to you?" I asked. "Why did you walk away like that?"

"I didn't particularly feel like being pelted with stones," Caleb retorted. "What happened to *you*? Why didn't you say anything?"

"What could I say, after what we saw?" I picked up a pebble and flicked it toward the river. Instead of skimming over the surface, it sank to the bottom. *Plunk.*

"We didn't *see* anything. We

got scared, and everybody started making things up." Caleb turned to face me. "You let the other scouts rattle you."

"They outnumbered us," I said. "How was I supposed to stand up to them?"

"If we're going to build a nation in the Promised Land," Caleb said, "we're going to have to learn how to stand up for ourselves, even when we're outnumbered."

I didn't say anything. I tried to skip another pebble. This one also *plunked* right to the bottom.

"Even my Caleb eyes can see that this situation isn't ideal," said Caleb. "We could have done without the earthquake-eclipse-army-of-giants incident."

I threw another pebble. *Plunk.* "Now the people will never believe that we can conquer the land," I said. "Or survive in it."

"But what about you?" Caleb asked. "Do *you* believe it?"

Caleb didn't try to make his case, as he had before. Instead, he sat quietly beside me, waiting for me to come up with my own answer. I thought about the shadow that had fallen over us, the shaking of the earth under our feet, my heart pounding as we ran away. I thought about the Israelites shouting, wielding stones. Then I thought about the burst of lush greenery at the edge of the dry desert, the feel of pomegranate seeds on my tongue, the sound of our laughter as the juice ran down our forearms.

"I wouldn't have believed we could be free after four hundred years," I began slowly, looking out over the river. "Or that the sea would part so that we could escape the Egyptians..."

"But that happened," Caleb said softly.

"I wouldn't have believed that God could appear to us at Sinai or that God would forgive us after we made the Golden Calf."

"But that happened too," Caleb nudged. "It all happened."

"And I never would have believed"—I turned to face Caleb—"that there were pomegranates that big."

"See?" Caleb laughed. "I'm not saying it won't be difficult. Or even terrifying. I'm just saying that it's possible. And that it'd be worth it."

"For the pomegranates," I chided.

"And the giant grapes," chuckled Caleb.

"Ugh, please don't use the word 'giant' anymore," I moaned.

"I won't," Caleb promised. "But seriously. The people are scared right now, but they know Moses trusts you. They'll listen to you. So what are you going to say?"

I stood up and brushed myself off. "I guess I'll say that we need to start looking at the Promised Land through our Caleb eyes."

"That's the spirit!" Caleb cheered. "Are you ready to go back and face the crowd?"

I picked up one last stone and tossed it toward the river. This time it skimmed across the surface—skipping once, twice, three times—leaving ripples in its wake. "I think so," I said.

Caleb held his hand out to where the Israelites were gathered. "Lead the way."

I started to walk, then stopped myself. "Wait!" I grabbed Caleb's arm. "Before we go, would you just stand here with me for a moment?"

Caleb smiled. "Of course I will."

I looked out over the river, trying my best to see what lay ahead of us. I didn't ignore the dry brush and the walled cities. We'd have to deal with them in due time. But I tried my best to look past them, to see the greenery that lay ahead: the promise of a brighter future, even if we had to fight for it.

"We're free," I whispered, elbowing Caleb in the ribs.

"A miracle," answered Caleb, rubbing his side.

CHAPTER SIXTEEN

Moses Turns Away

A STIRRING OUTSIDE THE TENT OF MEETING WAS RISING TO a crescendo. Moses looked up at his older brother, Aaron.

"What could they possibly want now?" Aaron asked.

"The same things they always want," Moses mumbled, rubbing a tear with the sleeve of his robe. The robe, praise God (and the women who did the mending), was still like new. Not that it had been so splendid when it was new. It was, after all, the robe of a poor shepherd. But Moses himself was not like new either. His brow had wrinkled, his back was bent, his arms had grown weary holding up the staff of God's wonders.

And now his sister was gone.

Their sister.

"We've just buried Miriam," Aaron grumbled. "They can't keep their whining and bellyaching to themselves for one day?" Aaron had always been adept at expressing himself. In Egypt, his skill had served them well in front of Pharaoh. Here in the desert, his constant gripes about the Hebrew people's attitudes, Moses's decisions, and occasionally even the actions of God were less useful—even when they were true. "Miriam was a prophetess, and this is how they mourn her death?" Aaron glared at the tent entrance.

Moses sighed and stood, leaning heavily on that staff he was coming to loathe. "Let's go see what they want." He opened the tent.

"We're thirsty!" the first dozen or so Hebrews shouted, as soon as the sunlight hit Moses's eyes.

Of course they were.

"We haven't had good water since Miriam died!"

Miriam had died only yesterday. The cisterns were still full. But Moses did not mention this.

"She was the source of water! Now that she's gone, we'll never find water again!"

They had complained just as much when Miriam was alive.

"Why did you bring us out of Egypt if we were only going to wander, thirsty and starving, for forty years? We could have just as easily died there!"

"Where there was water!"

"And meat!"

"And cucumbers!"

Cucumbers?! Moses turned to Aaron. "I'm sorry I don't know this, brother. Were cucumbers highly prized in Goshen?" They had been readily available at the palace, but Moses knew he couldn't take the luxury of his own circumstances in Egypt for granted.

Aaron snorted. "No. They're just complaining, Moses. As usual."

Anger was rising in Moses's throat. He pushed it down resolutely. These were his people, his flock. Once upon a time, he had handled crabby old goats with kindness and good cheer; he could surely keep doing that for crabby people.

As he had been doing.

For forty years.

Moses took a deep breath and imagined how his flock must feel about cucumbers. "Perhaps they miss them all the more keenly because they once took them for granted," he said to Aaron.

Aaron made a face at Moses, which Moses pretended not to see.

It was getting harder and harder to stay calm and patient. Moses knew there was a rage inside him. He had seen it at Sinai, when the people had made their golden idol, and before that, when he had killed the taskmaster. Moses was frightened of what he might do with his rage, so he strove to remain even-tempered. But even God got angry. In fact, it was often Moses's job to calm God down. The Hebrews would complain, about the lack of water, the taste of the miraculous manna that God gave them, or the miles of walking. God would threaten to destroy them all. Moses would remind God that the Hebrews were God's people, that God loved them, and that God would look pretty silly having brought them out of Egypt only to destroy them in the desert. Then God would provide manna, or water, or some sign of God's continued commitment to the Hebrew people, and all would be well. For a minute.

All will be well eventually, Moses reminded himself, even as he wished he could simply return to mourning for his sister—his sister, who had saved his life when he was a baby; Miriam, trusted prophetess of the Hebrew people, who had stood by his side and ministered to the flock with them, with a degree of patience Moses wished for at this moment.

Things hadn't been perfect between Moses and Miriam, of course. But was there a set of siblings that always got along? Moses hadn't found any, and his flock had thousands of sets of siblings.

"All right, friends, all right. I will ask God to provide water, as God has done many times before." Did his voice take on an edge when he said that? He hoped not.

Another member of his flock piped up. "Why did you even bring us out of Egypt, Moses?" It was their constant refrain. It was as if no one remembered the sting of the whip, the pangs of hunger, or all of the prayers to God begging God to get them out.

"Were there no more graves in Egypt, that you had to bring us out here to be buried?" another person called out.

There weren't any more, after Pharaoh filled them with your murdered infant sons, thought Moses. But he didn't say it.

Moses could feel his anger rising in him though. How many miracles did God have to perform before the Israelites would trust in God and stop complaining all the time? He opened his mouth, not sure what would come out of it, but Aaron pulled him back toward the tent. "Let's just talk to God, okay?" Moses took a deep breath. After all, if Aaron was the one calming Moses down, things were bad.

So they went into the Tent of Meeting. Moses and Aaron both fell on their faces. Moses could feel Aaron's shoulders shaking beside him, so he knew that Aaron, too, was crying. They remained on the ground with their faces in the dirt as God's presence surrounded them. God's voice was gentle and comforting. Clearly Moses was even angrier at the Hebrews right now than God was.

"Take My staff," God instructed Moses, "and gather My people. You and your brother Aaron shall speak to the rock in the presence of all of Israel, and they will see that it gives water."

They've seen me do it before and it's changed nothing, Moses thought but didn't say. Even though God could hear his thoughts and Moses knew that. Even though, if God was saying it would change this time, that meant it would.

Moses remained on the ground a few moments after God's presence receded. He needed time to calm down. He needed time just to be. To grieve. To breathe.

But there was never enough time. The people's angry voices rose, and Aaron came out of the trancelike state he usually went into in God's presence. Aaron looked at him and Moses nodded; he had their instructions. "God wants us to speak to the rock," he told Aaron.

Aaron rolled his eyes, but he stood and walked with Moses out of the tent.

The people started yelling when they saw the brothers, the same things they always yelled. "Egypt was a better place than this wasteland!"

"Where is our land of milk and honey, the land God promised?"

"Why did you lead us out to the desert just so we could die!"

Moses felt his face heating up, flaming red. Aaron, beside him, was growing agitated as well. A feeling of righteous fury was coming over Moses again.

Moses marched to the rock and smacked his staff against it. "You want Aaron and me to get you water from this rock?!" he bellowed at the gathered Hebrews. "You want me to raise my staff, perform the miracles you ask for, provide you with everything, only so you can complain some more?!"

Aaron doubled down. "All you people do is complain and whine and demand! Moses and Miriam and I, we have provided for you!" Moses could feel, under his rage, that there was something wrong with what he and Aaron were saying. But the rage was too powerful, too consuming, to pay any mind to that niggling feeling of doubt.

Moses slammed his staff against the rock again. "So here! Here it is! We have given you water! And I know we won't get a word of thanks!" Sure enough, water gushed from the rock onto the gathered crowd. Moses saw some faces light in joy, maybe even gratitude. But that doubtful feeling was still niggling at him as his rage abated. Moses knew that he had made a grave mistake. Aaron's eyes continued to blaze; he felt no doubt or guilt. But Moses knew. He had taken credit for God's miracle. He had claimed that they, and not God, had given the water. God would not be happy about this.

Sure enough, as soon as Moses entered the Tent of Meeting, he could feel God's presence. It wasn't comforting, as it had been before. It wasn't angry either, as Moses had expected. It was worse. It was disappointed.

"What did you do?" God asked.

Moses spoke, a little defensively. "I got water from the rock."

"No, Moses," God's voice said, heavy and sad. "*I* got water from the rock. You are acting as My instrument. It is supposed to be an honor."

Moses bowed his head. "I'm sorry." He could almost feel God sighing. "I know I misspoke. I am so tired, God. I have been leading the people for so long. I've mended squabbles. I've fought battles. I've held this staff until my arms have grown weary with it. And today, with Miriam gone...I just lost my temper."

God's presence had gone still. Moses heard, felt, saw nothing, for several moments. The air was so still, Moses wondered if his punishment had been rendered already, if this nothingness was what being struck dead by

God's wrath felt like. But the silence stretched on, and in it, Moses could feel his lungs grow and shrink as he inhaled and exhaled; he could feel his blood pulsing in his chest and his throat and his wrists. He wasn't dead, then. He shifted a bit and waited for God's verdict.

Finally, it came. "Moses: you and Aaron will not go into the Promised Land."

Anger flared at first in Moses's heart, then a deep sorrow. He would never see the Promised Land, this beacon of hope that God had been holding in front of him, in front of them all, for decades. He felt trepidation, too, over how Aaron would react to this news.

But beneath all of that, the strongest and most lasting emotion was relief.

"You claimed that you and Aaron, rather than I, provided the miracle of the water," God said. Moses could already hear Aaron huffing and puffing over this reason, which would sound to him like God was doing this just for God's ego. But Moses knew that wasn't it.

"My people cannot sustain themselves if they believe that you, and not I, are the source of their miracles, Moses," God said, heavily and gently. "You are both human, and you will die some day. If the Hebrews believe you to be the only reason they are together, the only reason they escaped Egypt and made it through the desert, your death will be the death of the very idea of the Hebrew people. They need Me, Moses. They need Me so that they can remain one people, My people. By taking credit for the water, you endanger the very existence of the Hebrew people. So I must deliver them into the Promised Land without you."

Moses took a deep breath, and as he exhaled, his sorrow and anger left him. All that remained in his heart was that sense of relief, to which he now gave voice. "God, it has been an honor to serve as Your conduit these many years. But to be honest, God, I am glad not to be leading the people into the Promised Land. I have been their leader out of Egypt, their leader for forty years of wandering. The Promised Land may flow with milk and honey. I am sure Your people will thrive once they are settled—but the settling will take more strength than I have left."

God's presence warmed and became comforting once again. "You have done so much, and you have done so well. It will not be easy to lead the Hebrews in the new land."

Moses laughed. "Yes, God. I'm aware of that." God's presence in that moment felt like a smile.

"Moses, you have done enough. You will lay down your staff before we reach the Promised Land, and you will be etched in the memory of the Hebrew people forevermore."

Moses stayed still on the sand for a little while, allowing God's presence to wrap around him like an embrace. Now that an end to that role had been assured, he felt calm and rested, prepared once again to fulfill his role, for whatever time he had left. He gathered himself and rose. God's presence hovered. "You know," Moses said, "Aaron is not going to be happy about this news."

At that, God laughed—a real, genuine laugh. Moses could feel and hear the rumble of it all around him. "Oh, Moses," God said. "When was the last time you saw Aaron happy?"

Moses laughed too. When God's presence receded, Moses left the tent again, to face the people, renewed in the knowledge that he had done all he could for the creation of the Jewish people.

CHAPTER SEVENTEEN

Why Curse When You Can Bless?

Jenny the donkey was worried about her future. If she'd been able to speak Human, she might have asked her master, Balaam the sorcerer, for advice.

Balaam had once made a good living telling fortunes and interpreting dreams. He had helped people talk to their relatives on the other side, as well as to the many gods people worshiped in Midian. There were many Midianites who would not begin a journey or make an important decision without first seeking his counsel.

But business had been slow for the last few years. Whereas before he couldn't keep up with the line of people waiting outside his house every day, now visitors to Balaam's home were few and far between. Either people had stopped seeking advice from sorcerers or they'd found others to consult.

Now Balaam was having trouble making ends meet. He'd sold off many of the finer things in his home and a few of his animals too. Jenny worried that she'd be next.

So when a caravan of King Balak's messengers arrived from Moab, it seemed like a stroke of good luck. Jenny brayed loudly to announce their arrival. Balaam rushed from the house, wearing the nicest robe he had left.

The messengers didn't waste time on pleasantries. "The Israelites have set up camp in Moab," said one messenger. "They have grown too numerous for the king's liking."

Jenny had heard of the Israelites. Some visitors had told incredible stories about a group of slaves that had escaped from Egypt. Their God had performed many miracles for them: splitting the sea, making food rain down from the sky, and lighting their path with a pillar of fire. Now the Israelites were making their way toward the land of Canaan, ready to defend themselves in battle against anyone who stood in their way. Lately, they had been on a winning streak.

"They fought King Sihon," said another messenger. "They defeated the Amorites. Now they are coming for Moab."

"King Balak has heard of your great power as a sorcerer," said the first. "He will pay you to curse the Israelites, so that he can defeat them."

This wasn't the first time someone had asked Balaam to curse an enemy. At the beginning, Balaam had refused these requests, saying that cursing people was a cowardly move. But his refusals only made people offer him more money, and ultimately Balaam gave in. Many of those curses had worked, and now the king of Moab wanted one too.

Balaam cleared his throat. "It is no small matter to curse an entire people...," he began.

"Name your price," said one messenger. "Money is no object." The other messenger groaned. If this was supposed to be a negotiation, it was over before it had begun.

Balaam stroked his long beard for a moment before throwing out a price so ridiculously high that Jenny never imagined that Balak's messengers would agree. But they accepted his fee without question. "Pack your things and get some sleep," they told him. "We'll come for you in the morning."

But Balaam did not sleep at all that night. He stayed up late, trying to summon a god or a demon that might curse the Israelites. He tried all of his usual methods: making offerings of fire to the different gods, casting dice and interpreting messages from their numbers. Nothing worked. Just when it appeared to Jenny that Balaam was about to drift off to sleep, a booming voice jolted both of them awake.

"Balaam son of Beor," the Voice thundered. "I am God of the Israelites. You must not go with these men to curse the Israelites. They are My people. And they are blessed."

Balaam looked shaken. While he often found divine messages from the dreams people shared or the way the dice fell on the table, this was the first time a god had spoken directly to him.

That didn't stop Balaam from arguing. "How can I refuse the king's summons?"

Or his money, Jenny added, but Balaam heard only a braying sound. He didn't speak Donkey.

The Voice did not soften, but the instructions changed. "If they have summoned you, you may go with them," the Voice declared. "But you may do only what I command you to do. Nothing more." The Voice paused. "And nothing less."

The next morning, Jenny felt Balaam's hands shaking as he fastened the saddle to her back. The messengers told Balaam to follow them to the Israelite camp. But the messengers' camels had longer legs than Jenny, and the two of them fell behind. Soon all they could see was the endless desert stretched out in front of them. Before they could catch up to the king's caravan, Jenny found herself blinded by a powerful light.

An angel was blocking their path.

When Balaam spoke of angels, Jenny imagined gauzy, glowing things that played the harp. But the being that blocked their path held a fiery sword and a stern expression, as if to say, *You shall not pass.*

Frightened, Jenny swerved into a ditch. She expected Balaam to be grateful that she'd saved his rump, but instead he smacked her hard on hers. He hadn't seen the angel, and now it had disappeared. Irritated, Balaam yanked on Jenny's reins, guiding them back onto the road.

They continued on in silence. Later, as they passed by a vineyard, the angel's bright light blocked Jenny's path once again. This time, she crashed into the vineyard wall. Balaam yelped as his foot smashed against the hard stones.

"Quit it!" he yelled, smacking Jenny again. She tried to move forward, but the angel was still standing there, fiery sword in hand. If Jenny went forward, they might both be killed. If she went off the road, Balaam might hit her again. So she did the only thing she could think of: she lay down in the middle of the road.

Balaam swore as he slid off Jenny's back and started to beat her with a stick. "Stupid donkey!" he yelled. "What's the matter with you?"

"What's the matter with me?!" Jenny brayed. "Don't you see the angel with the fiery sword?!"

Balaam jumped back in shock, dropping his stick. "You...you can talk?" he stammered.

Jenny opened her mouth again, not sure what kind of sound would come out: Human or Donkey. "I talk all the time," Jenny answered, as shocked as Balaam. "You can understand me?"

Balaam nodded, unable to speak.

"Well then, have a seat, buddy, because I've got something to say," Jenny said.

Still stunned, Balaam wordlessly obeyed.

"Why are you hitting me?" Jenny asked. "What have I ever done to you but help you out?"

Balaam took a moment to find his voice again. "You're making me look stupid in front of the king's men!"

Jenny looked toward the caravan, hundreds of yards ahead of them. "But we're *not* in front of the king's men, we're *behind* the king's men!"

"Ugh!" Balaam groaned. "You've just started talking, and now you make jokes? If I had a sword, I would kill you!"

"Whoa, calm down!" Jenny said. "How many trips have we been on together? Have I ever done this before?"

Balaam shook his head.

"Exactly. I'm trying to show you something."

This time, when Jenny nodded toward the angel, Balaam gasped. He bowed low to the ground, covering his face as the angel spoke.

"Balaam son of Beor!" the angel bellowed. "Why are you mistreating that poor donkey?"

Balaam hung his head, silenced once again.

The angel continued. "It was I who blocked your path, but only your donkey could see. God sent me to remind you that you cannot curse the Israelites. They are blessed. If you continue on this foolish mission, remember that you can say only what God tells you to say."

Balaam nodded in understanding and climbed up onto Jenny's back once again.

The angel stepped out of the way. "Now you may go."

"By the way," Jenny said, her voice already starting to sound more Donkey than Human again, "my name is Jenny."

Jenny thought that Balaam might turn them around and head home. But he continued to follow the messengers' caravan to Moab.

King Balak greeted them eagerly. "You can see part of the Israelite camp over that hill," he pointed. "Go curse them from there."

Jenny thought that Balaam might object. Instead, he told the king to prepare a sacrifice. Then he and Jenny rode over to the hill to look down at the Israelite camp. Jenny could see people darting in and out of a few makeshift tents. They didn't look very threatening. They looked like regular people doing regular people things: women kneading dough and baking bread; children throwing a ball back and forth and laughing.

One of the bread-bakers motioned to the ball-throwers as they ran by. She handed them a warm, fresh loaf and pointed to a tent on the far edge of camp. Jenny thought the children might devour the bread themselves before they reached their destination. But they ran cheerfully to the far-off tent, handing the bread to the elderly couple within.

Jenny nudged Balaam, trying to get her master to look at the Israelites more closely. But Balaam brushed her away. "We need the money, Jenny," he said. "I can't afford to have a king turn against me."

Jenny snorted but didn't speak.

By the time they returned to the king, Balaam was trembling. When he opened his mouth to speak to the king, Jenny noticed that Balaam's voice sounded different, as if it were coming from somewhere else.

"How can I curse someone God has not cursed?" he said softly, almost to himself. "What can I say against people who are not doomed?"

The king's face reddened. "What did you say?"

Balaam looked surprised at the words that were coming out of his mouth. Jenny wondered if that's what she'd looked like when she'd spoken Human. Balaam's voice grew louder.

"I look down on them from above.
They are too many to count—
as many as the dust of the earth."

"Stop!" the king shouted.

But Balaam kept speaking. "If only I could be as good as the Israelites! May my fate be like theirs!"

"I said stop!" The king stomped his foot on the ground. Balaam fell silent, looking as if the air had been let out of him. Jenny realized that he had stopped not because of the king's demands, but because he had finished saying what God had told him to say.

"I brought you here to curse my enemies!" the king fumed. "And now you've blessed them!"

"The angel was right." Balaam looked at Jenny as he gasped for breath. "I can do only as God tells me."

"God didn't hire you," the king scoffed. "Neither did this angel you're muttering about. I did! Now go curse them from over there!"

Balaam obeyed, riding Jenny toward the hill the king had pointed out. He stayed there for a long time, looking down on a different section of the camp. Here, a group of people had gathered in some kind of ritual. Though their accommodations were clearly not luxurious, they sang a beautiful melody giving thanks for their tents and sleeping mats, their simple meal and their well of water—a miraculous gift from God, they chanted.

Jenny looked over at Balaam, who seemed frozen in place. She couldn't tell if Balaam was waiting for God to speak to him or stalling because God had *already* spoken.

It was nearly sunset when they made their way back to the king. "The prophet returns!" he sneered. "Can you curse the Israelites now?"

Balaam pursed his lips together tightly, as if trying not to speak. But something forced them open, and the words poured out:

"God's mind does not change like ours does.
Who are we to challenge what God has chosen?
God freed them from Egypt with a mighty hand.
God is with them to this day!"

The king was furious. "Shut up!" he screamed. "Don't curse them *or* bless them!"

"I told you," Balaam sputtered. "I can do only as God tells me."

The two men stared at each other silently for a long time. The king looked as if smoke might come out of his ears. Balaam stood his ground, though Jenny could see that his hands were shaking.

Finally, still fuming, the king spoke. "I'm giving you one more chance," he said.

Third time's the charm, said Jenny. *Or the curse, I guess?*

But the men heard only braying.

From this third spot, they could see the entire Israelite camp. As Balaam stood beside her, Jenny saw thousands of tents arranged around one big tent, decorated with colorful embroidery like the finest saddle blanket.

"What am I going to do, Jenny?" Balaam groaned. "I can't go back there with another blessing. Even if he doesn't kill me or throw me in jail, no one will ever hire me as a sorcerer again. I'll be ruined!"

Jenny prayed that God would let her speak Human just one more time. "Forget about the king!" she said.

Balaam's head shot up in surprise. Jenny's prayer had been answered.

"Look at the Israelites." Jenny nodded toward the tents below them. "Forget the money. Forget your reputation. Just look at them. What do you *really* see?"

Jenny followed Balaam's gaze as he looked out over the cliff's edge at the Israelites. People were playing instruments and dancing, weaving cloth and pounding out tools from metal. Elders sat at the opening of their tents, teaching the children at their feet. Healers brought food and water to sick people on the edge of camp.

Balaam cleared his throat. "I see," he began, this time in his own voice, "people who stay strong and keep growing, even when everyone is against them. People who trusted God to lead them out of Egypt and kept believing through nearly forty years of wandering; who share with each other even when they barely have enough for themselves. People who teach their traditions to their children; who sing and dance even when life is hard. I see people who stay true to themselves, no matter what anyone else says or does."

Jenny tried to speak, but only Donkey sounds came out. So she nuzzled Balaam reassuringly instead.

"I can't curse these people." Balaam stood and brushed himself off. "Even if I could, I wouldn't want to. They are blessed. No matter what I say. No matter what anyone else says."

The king had worn a groove in the sand from pacing by the time Balaam and Jenny returned.

"Here comes the famous sorcerer!" the king spat. "Are you ready to curse them *now*?"

Balaam slid off Jenny's back and stood before the king. He didn't struggle or squirm as he had before, and there was a new kind of power in his voice. Though Jenny couldn't tell whether the words Balaam spoke came from God or not, she could see that Balaam felt in his heart that they were true.

"How lovely are your tents, O Jacob!
Your dwellings, O Israel!"

The king's face twisted with anger, turning a deep, purply red. But Balaam kept speaking. He said that the Israelites would grow as tall and fruitful as the sturdiest trees and that their leaders would be as fierce and proud as lions. Just as the king opened his mouth to shout, "Stop!" Balaam delivered the final blow:

"Those who bless them will be blessed.
Those who curse them will be cursed."

The king screamed with rage and stormed off toward where his men had tied their camels. "I hope this Israelite God gives you a hefty reward," he said. "Because you won't see one silver shekel from me!"

Jenny thought the king's threat might change Balaam's tune. Surely, having thwarted the king's plan would ruin his reputation as a sorcerer. But Balaam stood tall and proud by her side as the king and his caravan disappeared from view.

"Come on, Jenny," he said, climbing back into the saddle. "Let's go home."

As they rode back to Midian, Jenny tried to tell Balaam that she was proud of him, that he'd done the right thing. But she found she could only speak Donkey. So instead she waited patiently for Balaam to tell her what he was thinking.

"I don't know if anyone will ever hire me as a sorcerer again," Balaam said quietly. "But even if they do, I'm not going to curse people anymore. Cursing is a coward's move. I'd much rather give a blessing."

Jenny brayed in approval, and Balaam continued, "I think I'll send a blessing to the king, that he learn to see the good in people. Like I did, thanks to you."

Jenny's heart swelled with pride. She couldn't speak Human anymore, but she didn't think she'd need to. Balaam seemed to have found the right words on his own.

CHAPTER EIGHTEEN

Sisters Stand Up for Justice

HAVING FOUR SISTERS IS NO LAND OF MILK AND HONEY.

We shared everything, and there wasn't much to share. Nearly forty years ago, our parents had walked out of Egypt with the clothes on their backs, a pocketful of flat, dry matzah, and the earrings in my mother's ears. It was miracle enough that the five of us, born in the desert, had any clothing at all.

We spent our days trudging through the sand, trying not to step on each other's heels. Someone—usually my sister Noa—was always shouting, "Hurry up!" And someone—usually my sister Machlah—was always panting, "Wait for me!"

At night, we squished into one tiny tent, where we lay on the hard ground and fought over the covers. My sister Milcah kicked me in the shins as she tossed and turned. My sister Tirza talked in her sleep. I loved my sisters, but sometimes I also hated them. I'm pretty sure the feeling was mutual.

What I hated most was when people would mix us up. Our aunts, uncles, and cousins—there were *so* many cousins—would sometimes yell out "Machlah-Milcah-Noa-Tirza" before finally settling on my actual name, Hoglah. It was as if we were interchangeable. Only my father always seemed to know when it was me.

Being a girl already made me feel invisible most of the time. The men in our tribe insisted we stay covered from head to toe out of modesty. Given that we spent long days under the hot desert sun, this wasn't as impractical as it sounded. But sometimes it seemed they didn't want to hear our voices any more than they wanted to see our faces.

The Elders made all the decisions for their tribes, and all of them were older men. Younger men trained to fight in battle or serve in the Tent of Meeting. And my sisters and me? We did whatever the brothers we didn't have would have done, along with everything else expected of women. We set up our tent and took it down whenever we moved. We gathered manna, drew water, chased away wild animals. We repaired sandals and mended clothing for ourselves and our cousins—there were *so* many cousins. All without being seen or heard—all without mattering.

We worked day and night, doing all the little things the Elders never considered important. One day they declared it a miracle that their clothes hadn't worn out during the forty years we had wandered in the desert. Of course their clothes hadn't worn out! The women had taken the men's garments from their tents each night and patched them back together by firelight. But like the women who had sewn them, the seams of our work were invisible.

If one daughter was invisible, five daughters were considered bad luck. But my father didn't think so. He always valued us, never told us he wished we were boys. "I have everything I need," he used to say when he looked at us. "You remind me so much of your mother."

We did our best to stay positive, even after our mother died, because we knew our wandering had a purpose. God had promised us that our people would one day live in a land that was lush and green, spacious and wide. Each tribe was promised a piece of *that* land. Each clan was promised a piece of *that* land. Each family was promised a piece of *that* land, and each person in that family would get a piece of *that* land.

I dreamed of building a house on my own patch of land—of planting fruits and vegetables, raising sheep and goats. I could pass that land down to my children, who would never have to share with *their* sisters, or their brothers if they had them, or their cousins. With four aunts, there would certainly be a lot of cousins, even more than we already had!

My sisters and I tried to be patient and agreeable as our years of wandering drew to a close. Noa and I woke up early to gather our manna for breakfast. Machlah and Milcah helped set up our tent whenever we moved. Tirza didn't fuss when one of our cousins—there were *so* many cousins—burst into our tent unannounced, knocking over our water jars and soaking our blankets.

Then our father died, and everything got harder. People harassed my sisters and me and even stole from our water supply, knowing we had no one to come to our defense. The only bright spot was daydreaming about living on our father's patch of the Promised Land, something that no one could take away from us.

When Moses announced that the Promised Land lay just beyond the river, I shouted for joy. "Can you imagine?" I gushed to my sisters. "Having our own homes in our own land?" I could nearly taste the sweet honey I would press from the dates in my someday-soon backyard.

"I'm going to plant rows of grapevines and pomegranates," Tirza declared.

"And an almond tree right in front of the house, so that I can watch it bloom every year when the winter is over," Noa said.

Milcah and Machlah were picking out colors for the rugs they would weave when a few of our cousins interrupted. There were so many cousins, almost all of them men, and they were always interrupting.

"Land?" one cousin laughed. "You aren't getting any land!"

I dug my fists into my sides so I wouldn't punch him in the stomach. "What do you mean, we aren't getting any land?"

"God gave this land to the Israelite *men*," he explained. "To pass down to their sons."

"But our father didn't have any sons!" Tirza cried.

"We know," a second cousin chimed in. "Your father's land will go to the men in the family."

"And that's us," the first cousin said smugly. "It's the law God gave to Moses!"

Now it felt like *I* had been punched in the stomach. "You mean that we've been wandering for our entire lives, putting up with each other and all of you, even when we're hot and tired and dirty and cranky, for *nothing*?!"

"Not nothing," said the first cousin. "You can always come live with us."

"*If* we have room," the second cousin sneered. Then they both turned on their heels and left us in a cloud of dust.

For so long, I had tried to cooperate. I didn't complain when our cousins hogged the manna or when our aunts played their timbrels late into the night when I was trying to sleep. But now the anger bubbled up inside of me. The words I had been longing to say throughout our years of wandering came tumbling out on a wave of tears. "That's...*not*...FAIR!"

"Hoglah's right," Noa said, putting her hand on my shoulder. "We've been wandering just as long as everyone else."

Tirza nodded in agreement. "We deserve the land just as much as they do."

"It's not our fault we don't have any brothers," Milcah said.

"Right," said Machlah. "It's not like we could have done anything to change that!"

"It's *not* fair," Tirza repeated. "But what can we do about it?"

"Yeah," Noa said. "It's not like we can ask Moses to change God's law."

My head snapped up at Noa's words. I looked out toward the center of camp, where the Elders gathered each day to settle disputes about the law. My heart began to pound. "That's *exactly* what we are going to do."

"Are you nuts?!" Noa sputtered.

I shook my head.

Milcah turned her gaze toward the Elders' meeting space. "There has to be another way."

"Like what?" Machlah asked. "Hoping our cousins will take us in?"

Tirza laughed bitterly. "It would be better than getting kicked out altogether."

"Would it?" My voice had a sharp edge. For a long time, my sisters and I stood facing one another, not saying a word. My breath was heavy and wet from crying. For what felt like forty years, I waited for one of us to say something. But when the silence became too much to bear, I turned around and started walking.

For one terrifying moment, I imagined confronting the Elders alone. Then I heard a set of sandaled feet fall into step with mine, and then another. Even without looking over my shoulder, I felt my sisters following behind me. In that moment, I loved knowing that there were five of us.

By the time we reached the center of camp, the afternoon sun beat down on our tired bodies. I wanted to squeeze one of my sisters' hands, just to know that I wouldn't melt away into nothing, but my hands were sweating and shaking too much.

We found the Elders right where we knew they'd be, sitting in a circle, discussing some part of God's law as a crowd of people looked on. I took a deep breath before saying, in a loud clear voice, "My sisters and I have a dispute to settle."

The Elders kept talking among themselves. The rest of the crowd ignored us.

"Um, excuse me?" nudged Noa.

Tirza tried next. "Pardon?"

"Could we have a moment of your time?" Milcah and Machlah managed.

But no one was listening. Maybe we really *were* invisible. Or at least inaudible.

Noa tugged at my skirt and nodded to her left, where a large camel was tied to a tent post. Together we made our way toward the giant beast. Machlah and Milcah hoisted me up onto the camel's hump. I smoothed my skirts, sat up straight, and shouted at the top of my lungs. "It's... *not* ... FAIR!"

The Elders fell quiet. They turned their bearded faces toward the camel, staring at us with questioning eyes.

"You must be lost," one of them said dismissively, stroking his long white beard.

"We aren't lost," Noa said.

Tirza chimed in. "We are exactly where we need to be."

My sisters looked up at me expectantly. I cleared my throat and began to speak. "My name is Hoglah," I said. "Daughter of Zelophechad. And these are my sisters: Machlah, Milcah, Noa, and Tirza."

"We were born in the wilderness," Milcah's voice rang out clearly. "Our parents died here. We have no brothers."

"We've been wandering the desert for our entire lives," Machlah said, planting her feet firmly in the sand. "But now that we are about to enter the Promised Land, our cousins tell us that our father's land will go to them, simply because we are daughters, not sons."

Hearing my sisters speak made me feel strong enough to say the hardest words of all. "I know God gave this law to Moses, but it isn't fair. If our father's land goes to our cousins, his name and his memory will be lost forever. My sisters and I will have nothing to live on."

The Elders looked at me, then at my sisters, standing tall beside the camel. They looked back at each other. But no one said a word.

It was a man's voice that shattered the silence. "She's right!" he exclaimed. "That's *not* fair."

I looked up to see Moses himself standing at the edge of the sea of people, staring right at me. The crowd parted like the Sea of Reeds as Moses walked toward the camel. "All that you have said is true," he agreed. "It isn't fair that you can't inherit your father's land."

The Elders looked on with shocked expressions as Moses helped me down from the camel. "But this is God's law," one Elder said sternly.

"We've never changed a law from God before."

"Then we'll have to ask God to change it," Moses told him matter-of-factly. "After all, how can these sisters take care of themselves, and each other, if they have nowhere to live?"

The Elders watched in astonishment as Moses disappeared into the Tent of Meeting to plead our case before God. My sisters and I made a circle in the sand and stood there, waiting for our fate to be decided.

We stayed there in that circle for what seemed like another forty years. Just when it felt like our legs might buckle beneath us, Moses emerged with his answer: "God has told me that your cause is just. The law must be changed. That way your sisters, and all the daughters that come after you, will always have a place to build, plant, and grow in the Promised Land."

My sisters and I drew Moses into a hug. There was quite a lot of walking and waiting, building and planting still to do. But we would do it together.

"You were right to speak out. You did a brave thing," Moses told me. "Now your father's name will be remembered forever."

When we finally crossed over into the Promised Land, my sisters and I inherited our father's land. Like everything else we'd ever had, we split it between us. My portion was a little smaller than the others. But there was a stream and a date palm for pressing honey and, soon enough, my very own house.

No one kicked me in my sleep anymore. My cousins came only when they were invited. There was no more manna or magical springs. Now we had to work for our food. But we were happier than we had ever been.

That day God gave one more gift to me and my sisters, because we had stood up for what was right. God told Moses to write down each of our names next to the new law, so that no one would ever forget them again.

CHAPTER NINETEEN

The Remembering Song

A FEW WEEKS BEFORE THE ISRAELITES WERE SUPPOSED TO cross the Jordan River, Moses called Joshua into his tent. He didn't pull any punches. He didn't even say hello. "I won't be going up to the Promised Land with you," he said. "It's time for you to lead the Israelites."

Usually Moses stuttered when he spoke, but today it was Joshua's words that felt slow in coming. "But you...you've led us for decades," Joshua stammered. "What...why would you abandon us now?"

Moses winced at the word "abandon." "This isn't my decision to make," he said. "God told me that I will die here in the wilderness, along with the rest of the generation that left Egypt."

Joshua knew that entering the Promised Land was a privilege not given to most of their peers. Because of their panicked reaction to the scouts' reports of giants in the Promised Land, the generation that left Egypt was condemned to wander the wilderness until they died out. Only Joshua and Caleb, who had rejected the fearmongering of their fellow scouts, were permitted to cross over.

Never for a second had Joshua thought this meant that Moses, too, would die in the wilderness, leaving Joshua to lead this new generation of Israelites into the Promised Land alone.

Joshua began to sweat, his throat dry, his heart pounding. "But why?"

"Because I lost my temper and struck the rock. Because I took credit for God's miracle." Moses went down the list. It all seemed pretty small to Joshua, in light of all the good that Moses had done in his lifetime. "Besides," Moses added, "I'm getting too old. It's your turn."

Joshua laughed in disbelief. "And I'm so young and energetic?!" He was only a few years younger than Moses. The people they had grown up with, left Egypt with, and wandered with for all these years had started to die off. Their children were grown-ups now, mirror images of the parents they'd outlived, training to serve in the army that would conquer the Promised Land. Often Joshua called them by their parents' names, forgetting that he was an old man and that most of his friends were gone.

"God has chosen you to lead this people after me," said Moses. "You've proved yourself to be a leader on the battlefield and in other ways too. You've been preparing for this your whole life."

"Have I?" Joshua remembered the times he'd been given the chance to lead. They hadn't exactly gone well. Back when Joshua and Caleb had stood up to their fellow scouts, the Israelites had threatened to pelt them both with stones. Whatever battles Joshua had won had been because Moses had been standing on the sidelines, his arms outstretched, cheering him on. Joshua couldn't imagine that Moses wouldn't be there for the next battle or the many that came after it.

"And don't forget," Moses added, "God is going with you, to guide you."

This raised a whole new specter of worries for Joshua. Moses had always been the one to speak with God, face-to-face, as no other human being had ever done. Each time Moses left God's presence, his face would glow so brightly that he had to cover it with a veil. Moses was able to go weeks without food or water when he was on the mountain with God. "Will I be able to speak to God as you have?" Joshua asked.

"Everyone's relationship with God is different," Moses said. "You will talk to each other in your own way."

Joshua didn't find this very reassuring. But when he tried to formulate another question, all that came out was "How...?"

Moses drew Joshua close to him, placing his hands on Joshua's head, a gesture of blessing. "Be brave, and be strong," he said. "You'll figure it out. I promise."

The two men stood there in silence for a long while. Joshua stared into Moses's eyes, searching for some hint of the wisdom that Moses had gathered in his lifetime. But all he saw was his own reflection as Moses stared back at him. And was that fear in Moses's eyes or sadness?

"What about you?" Joshua asked. "What's going to happen to you?"

"The same thing that happens to all of us eventually." Moses looked down at his hands. "We grow old, and God gathers us in to be with our ancestors. We always wish that we had more time, but we hope we've done enough that our legacy lives on. That those who come after us will keep moving forward. That they'll remember..." His eyes filled with tears.

This time, Joshua drew Moses close. Joshua was used to being Moses's helper. Now Moses was telling him to be the leader. Joshua didn't know where to begin. He didn't even know how to stop Moses from crying.

"We won't forget you, Moses," Joshua promised. "We'll tell your story to our children and our children's children."

Moses stiffened. "I'm not worried about me," he said, though Joshua didn't quite believe him. "I'm worried about *you*."

Joshua laughed again. "I'm worried about me too."

"Not you—*you*," Moses corrected, waving his hand in a large arc at the Israelite camp surrounding them. "I'm worried that you, the Israelites, will forget the Teaching. I'm worried about what will happen the next time the people get into trouble."

Joshua was worried about that too. The Israelites had rebelled many times: building the Golden Calf; begging to return to Egypt; complaining, every day it seemed, that they were hungry, tired, and thirsty. When God had threatened to destroy them, Moses argued for them to have another chance. With Moses gone, would they be out of chances?

"When I'm gone," Moses told him, "the Israelites will forget the covenant we made at Mount Sinai. They'll follow the wrong people and go after the wrong things. They'll get kicked out of the land you fought so hard for. They'll be scattered all over the earth. They'll forget what matters, and I won't be there to remind them." Moses looked at Joshua, then looked away. "And someday, you won't be either."

That night, Joshua couldn't sleep. In those rare moments when he drifted off, he dreamed of all the things that could possibly go wrong. When he lay awake, he thought of everything that had *already* gone wrong. The Israelites could be stubborn and fickle, seeing a miracle with their own eyes one moment and saying, moments later, that God had abandoned them. How would they ever remember all the laws and stories in the Teaching?

As he tossed and turned, he thought of Moses's blessing. *Be brave and be strong.* It reminded him of a song his mother used to sing him when he couldn't sleep. Even though she had long since passed away, he'd never forgotten the melody. His mother had always been adding new verses, but the chorus was always the same.

Remember I love you, even when I'm not here.
Remember, my love, there's no reason to fear.
Be brave, and be strong.
And don't forget the Remembering Song.

Joshua sat up and poked his head out of his tent. Light was spilling over the horizon, turning the night sky a bluish gray. Joshua walked quickly across the camp to Moses's tent, humming along the way.

Moses didn't seem surprised at all to see Joshua so early in the morning. He clearly hadn't been sleeping either. But he did find Joshua's request strange. "You want us to do *what*?!"

"You're worried that the people won't remember the Teaching after we're gone," Joshua explained. "What if we taught them a song to help them remember?"

"I don't know." Moses shook his head. "That sounds kind of silly."

"It might be," Joshua admitted. "But think of all the songs we learned when we were little. They stay with us. If we teach them a song, they'll teach it to their children, and so on and so on. It will get stuck in their heads…"

"Like the songs Miriam taught us." Moses smiled, remembering his sister.

Joshua knew he had made his point. "Come on," he said. "We don't have much time."

They worked on the song all the next day and through the following night. When the sun came up again, they were exhausted but pleased. Moses sounded the shofar, and the Israelites gathered at the entrance to the Tent of Meeting.

"It is time for you all to go ahead into the Promised Land," Moses told them. "I will remain here. God has chosen Joshua to lead you forward from now on."

Gasps and murmurs were heard from the crowd. The people who had once doubted Joshua were no longer around, but some of their misgivings had clearly been passed on to their children.

Moses hushed the people by placing his hands on Joshua's head, blessing him for everyone to see. Joshua looked at the ground, his face flushed. Once again, he heard Moses say, "Be brave and be strong."

"Joshua is thoughtful and courageous. He will be a good leader," Moses continued. "But we can't always count on just one leader. We need all of you to play a part in making sure we don't forget our covenant with God."

Joshua stepped forward. "This song will remind us of the most important parts of the Teaching. Whenever we're not sure what to do, we can sing it to ourselves. And we'll teach it to our children too," Joshua said, "so that they'll know what to do after we're gone."

Joshua began to hum the melody, and Moses hummed along. The Israelites looked puzzled at first, but one by one they started humming along, too, as if they couldn't help it.

Moses and Joshua taught them the words, verse by verse, singing a line for the Israelites to repeat, the same way they'd sung with Miriam when the sea split.

Let the words come down like rain,
We'll sing it once and twice and again.

Chorus: Be brave, and be strong;
And don't forget the Remembering Song.

God is our Rock, sturdy and strong,
And promised our years in this land would be long.

Remember the story our ancestors told:
Teach it to the young, learn it from the old.

We were slaves. God set us free
With plagues and a path through the splitting sea.

In the wilderness, there was manna to eat,
Clothes on our back, and shoes on our feet.

God created us; God set us apart
And told us to carry these words in our heart.

This is the way that God wants us to live:
When we're wrong, we say sorry. When we're right, we forgive.

We love God, and each other, through acts that are kind.
What hurts and what heals are what we keep in mind.

We'll make mistakes, as people and as a nation,
And learn to do better, in each generation.

God's face might be hidden; God's voice might be low,
But God will be with us, wherever we go.

Our words matter; our deeds matter,
Even if someday our people are scattered.

Chorus: Be brave, and be strong;
And don't forget the Remembering Song.

They practiced the song all day and into the early evening. Then Joshua sent everyone back to their tents. "We have a long journey ahead of us. Go get some rest."

When the crowd had dispersed, Joshua turned to Moses. "Do you think it will work?"

"Shh," Moses said. "Listen."

Joshua shut his eyes and listened to the sounds of sandals on the ground as the Israelites walked back to their tents. He heard the noise made by the kindling of fires, the clanging of pots and pans, the chatter of neighbors inviting each other into their homes. He hadn't really noticed it before, but the camp had its own kind of music.

And floating over it all was the sound of hundreds of children singing. Not quite all together. Not even quite at full voice. But singing, quietly to themselves, as if they couldn't help it:

Our words matter, our deeds matter,
Even if someday our people are scattered.
Be brave, and be strong
And don't forget the Remembering Song.

CHAPTER TWENTY

The Crowns on the Letters

MOSES LET OUT A HEAVY SIGH AS HE WROTE DOWN THE final words of the Torah. It felt as if every one of his 120 years had been written on his body with a chisel. He ached all over. Soon, though, he would be finished.

Not that he hadn't enjoyed writing the Torah. Speaking was often hard for him. But Moses found that words flowed easily from his fingers, old though they were, onto the parchment. His handwriting grew neat and precise as he wrote down the stories of his people and the rules God had given them.

But God was a stickler for detail. Just when Moses thought he was finished, God laid out one last task for him. Each time he saw the letter *gimmel*, *zayin*, *tet*, *nun*, *ayin*, *tzadi*, or *shin*, Moses was to add three tiny lines that looked like a crown.

At first Moses loved watching the letters sprout beautiful flourishes under his quill. But then his arm grew tired. There were so many! His fingers cramped. Hours of squinting against the desert sun made the tiny letters blur before his aging eyes.

Moses called out to God, "This is taking *forever*!" He massaged the palm of his writing hand with his other thumb. "Why do we need to put fancy little crowns on these tiny little letters? They don't *mean* anything."

"Maybe to *you*, they don't mean anything," God corrected. "But they'll mean something to the generations that come after you."

Moses must have looked as perplexed as he felt, because God went on to explain. "You've seen for yourself that the world is always changing."

"Isn't that the truth?" Not all of the changes had felt good when they happened. Some of them still didn't.

God continued, "That means future generations will ask questions we haven't thought of yet."

How could there be questions God hasn't thought of yet? Moses wondered to himself. *Isn't God all-knowing?*

"I know what you're thinking," God chided, startling Moses. "I could make some predictions. But your generation wouldn't understand them. I mean, do you know what a smartphone is?" Moses shook his head. "So if I explained to you how to use one, even though you wouldn't see one for almost three thousand years, wouldn't it be a waste of space in the Torah?"

Moses had to agree that it would be. The scroll was already quite heavy. *How could we carry it from place to place if it held the answers to questions that hadn't been asked yet?*

"But why will we need to ask more questions?" Moses asked. "Why can't we keep things the way they are now?"

"You realize you just asked two questions, right?" God teased.

Moses groaned in frustration.

"Think of the stories you just wrote down," said God. "Many of them started with a question. Like Adam and Eve asking, 'What happens if we eat this fruit?'"

"That didn't turn out so well," said Moses.

"Would you be here if they hadn't?" God pressed.

Moses had never thought of it that way before. "I guess not."

"Think about when you were a baby," God continued. "The midwives, your mother, your sister, Pharaoh's daughter—they all asked the same question: 'Why should this child not have a chance to live, simply because he is a Hebrew?' See how that turned out?"

Moses smiled, remembering both of his mothers.

"You've asked a lot of questions too," God said.

Like, Why me? Moses thought.

"Exactly," God laughed. Moses wished for the thousandth time he could describe God's laugh in words. "You've asked, *Why me?* so many times. But you've also asked, *Why are the Hebrews treated differently from the Egyptians?* Isn't that question the reason we've come this far?"

Moses had to admit that it was.

"Questions help us change the world," God continued. "Even thousands of years from now, people will return to this book with new questions."

Moses found that hard to believe. "Can You show me?"

God told Moses to close his eyes and turn around. Moses obeyed, feeling the air around him grow wavy and thick, as if he were swimming underwater.

When he opened his eyes, the mountain beneath Moses's feet had vanished. Suddenly he stood in the back of a classroom where a group of young people were bent over their books.

"Where are we?" Moses whispered, not believing his eyes. "*When* are we?"

"Jerusalem," God answered. "More than a thousand years from now. The teacher's name is Akiva."

Moses faced Akiva and tried to listen. The room buzzed with questions, flying in every direction like a swarm of bees. Sometimes Akiva would explain a law or custom that Moses had never heard of. Other times Akiva would respond to a question with *another* question, and the buzzing would start all over again.

Moses recognized a word here and there. *God. Shabbat. Torah. Israel.* He heard Akiva say, "Love your neighbor as yourself," and that made him smile. But there was a lot he didn't understand. He felt as if he were swimming through that thick, wavy air again.

"What does all of this *mean*?" Moses wondered aloud.

The students all swiveled in their chairs to look at Moses. He hadn't realized that they could hear him or see him.

"Did you have a question?" Akiva asked. "We *love* questions!"

"I can see that!" Moses said. "But where did all these questions come from?"

"Oh, that's an easy one," said Akiva. "They came from our teacher

Moses, who wrote down God's Torah on Mount Sinai. We found them in the crowns on the letters."

Moses could practically hear God saying, *See, I told you!* "So you and your students must know everything there is to know, then, right?"

"Not quite." Akiva laughed and shook his head. "I don't know why the *alef* in the word *vayikra* is little or why the *dalet* in the word *echad* is big. I don't know whether all life on earth was really created in six days or whether it evolved over a million years..."

"Do you know what a smartphone is?" Moses asked hopefully.

"A what?" Akiva looked puzzled. "No, I don't. And I don't know what the world will look like in two thousand years, and what questions students will be asking then..."

"God?" Moses had a question of his own. "Will people really still be reading the Torah and asking new questions two thousand years from now?"

"Absolutely!" God replied. "In every generation, there will be new students reading the laws and stories of the Torah and seeing what they can learn. The world they live in will look completely different from the world each of you lives in. They will have some of the same questions that you have now, and new ones too. Like you, they'll follow My teachings and traditions and pass them on. Like you, they'll create their own customs and pass on their own ideas too. And like you, they'll ask the most important question: How can we make the world better?"

Akiva and Moses looked at each other. God guessed their question, even though they hadn't asked it aloud. "Close your eyes and turn around."

Moses and Akiva closed their eyes and turned around. The air felt wavy and thick. When they opened their eyes, they were right here in this room, waiting to meet *you*, the next link in the never-ending chain of our people. They were waiting to hear the questions *you* will ask, the answers *you* will discover, and the stories *you* have to tell.

Discussion Guide

Whether you read these stories just for fun, use them for learning and teaching, or both, the resources on the following pages can help guide exploration and discussion of the stories. Use it on your own, with a partner, or in a group or class.

The first section introduces some essential Jewish values—sometimes called *midot*—that connect to the stories in this book. Under each value, we've listed a few stories you might want to read to see that value in action. The next section provides questions for discussion and reflection about each story. And the last section is an index of the biblical, rabbinic, and contemporary sources for and values in each story.

Values Guide

B'TZELEM ELOHIM · In the Image of God

In the Creation story, we learn that all human beings are created *b'tzelem Elohim*, "in the image of God" (Genesis 1:26–27). This doesn't literally mean we look like God, as we don't know what God looks like. Rather, it means we all have the ability to be like God in some way—for instance, to be creative like God, to be kind like God, to be fair like God. Everyone we encounter is, in some way, a reflection of God's image, and we must treat all people as if they have the potential to be like God.

- *Maybe It Happened This Way* (page 1)
- *A Matter of Life and Death* (page 67)
- *Standing, Sitting, and Signing at Sinai* (page 103)

CHESED · Kindness

The ancient rabbi Shimon the Righteous said, "On three things the world stands: on study [*Torah*], on prayer [*avodah*], and on acts of loving-kindness [*g'milut chasadim*]" (*Pirkei Avot* 1:2). These are the actions we take to show others that we care about them, actions such as visiting the sick, listening to people who are sad or scared, and helping people or animals who are hungry, thirsty, or tired. Another word we sometimes use for kindness is *rachamim*, which means "mercy" or "compassion."

- *Rebecca Goes Forth* (page 33)
- *Sisters Stick Together* (page 47)
- *Please, God, Heal Her* (page 129)

EMET · Truth

Life and learning might be much easier if everyone could agree on one version of the truth. But there is usually more than one side to a story. This is true of the Torah as well. Some rabbis say that there are "seventy faces of the Torah" (Numbers Rabbah 13:15–16), meaning that any part of our sacred story can be interpreted seventy different ways—at least!

A fun fact about the word *emet*: It is made up of the first, middle, and last letters of the Hebrew *alef bet*, which reminds us to tell "the whole truth."

- *Maybe It Happened This Way* (page 1)
- *Adam and Eve Grow Up* (page 5)
- *Go Forth and Smash the Idols!* (page 25)

EMUNAH · Faith

The word *amen*, said at the end of a prayer, comes from the same root as the Hebrew word *emunah*. It is a way of telling the prayer leader, "I believe in what you just said." Having faith means believing in something—God, our community, or ourselves—even without proof or absolute certainty and even when it is challenging or painful.

- *Go Forth and Smash the Idols!* (page 25)
- *Dancing on the Shores of the Sea* (page 95)
- *Seeing through Caleb Eyes* (page 137)

HIDUR MITZVAH · Making Our Traditions Beautiful

It isn't always enough to do something "right"; sometimes we need to put extra thought into it, to make it special too. Being a part of a Jewish community is meant to be both beautiful and joyful, although sometimes it's also a lot of work!

- *Dancing on the Shores of the Sea* (page 95)
- *(Don't) Give Up Your Gold!* (page 111)
- *The Crowns on the Letters* (page 185)

K'HILAH K'DOSHAH · Sacred Community

K'hilah comes from a Hebrew word meaning "to gather or assemble." Communities are a huge part of Jewish life, and they're made up of many different kinds of people and families. Being a *k'hilah k'doshah*, a sacred community, means making sure everyone feels welcome to participate in the community. It means celebrating our differences, the things that make each of us unique.

- *Standing, Sitting, and Signing at Sinai* (page 103)
- *Moses Turns Away* (page 149)
- *Why Curse When You Can Bless?* (page 157)
- *The Remembering Song* (page 177)

L'DOR VADOR · From Generation to Generation

Dor means "generation" in Hebrew, and the phrase *l'dor vador* means "from generation to generation." So much of our tradition depends on passing down customs and knowledge to the next generation, even if those customs evolve over time. In the V'ahavta prayer, which comes from the Torah, we say, *V'shinantam l'vanecha*, "You shall teach them to your children" (Deuteronomy 6:7). We need each new generation to take responsibility for carrying our ancestors' teachings and traditions into the future.

- *Noah's Hope* (page 17)
- *The Remembering Song* (page 177)
- *Crowns on the Letters* (page 185)

OMETZ LEIV · Courage

Ometz leiv means "strength of heart." Many people in our sacred story had to take their own paths even when everyone around them was going in a different direction. They may have believed something different from their peers, imagined a different life for themselves, or felt compelled to stand up for what they knew was right. These actions require courage. This means doing the right thing even when no one else agrees. The Yiddish word *chutzpah* also means "courage" or "nerve." You might not want to have *too* much chutzpah, but sometimes we need a little bit to make change in the world!

- *A Matter of Life and Death* (page 67)
- *Miriam Saves Her Brother* (page 75)

- *Sisters Stand Up for Justice* (page 169)
- *The Remembering Song* (page 177)

PIKUACH NEFESH · Saving a Life

Because we are created in God's image (see *b'tzelem Elohim*), every human life is precious. Our tradition teaches us that we must think of both our own life and health and the life and health of our loved ones whenever we make important decisions. Some people in the Torah took great risks in order to save lives, including defying the orders of Pharaoh in Egypt.

- *A Matter of Life and Death* (page 67)
- *Miriam Saves Her Brother* (page 75)

SH'LOM BAYIT · Peace in the Home

We see many different kinds of families in the stories of the Torah, and not everyone gets along. Some conflicts end with someone getting hurt or with family members not being able to live or work together. Other times family members work hard to look past their differences and heal their hurts so that there can be *sh'lom bayit*—peace in the home.

- *Rebecca Goes Forth* (page 33)
- *Sisters Stick Together* (page 47)
- *Standing at the Edge of the Pit* (page 55)

TIKVAH · Hope

Throughout our people's long history, there have been many times when we have been exiled, oppressed, or persecuted. Still we have persevered, survived, and thrived in the face of many challenges. This is in part because we have always held onto the hope that life can get better. During one of the darkest times in our history—when the Temple was destroyed and we were exiled from the Land of Israel—the prophet Jeremiah reminded our people, "There is hope for your future" (Jeremiah 31:17).

The word *tikvah* is central to the Israeli national anthem, "Hatikvah," meaning "The Hope." The words remind us of our long-held dream to return to the Land of Israel.

- *Noah's Hope* (page 17)
- *Dancing on the Shores of the Sea* (page 95)
- *Seeing through Caleb Eyes* (page 137)

T'SHUVAH · Fixing Our Mistakes

T'shuvah means "to turn" or "to return." Sometimes in life, we go in the wrong direction and hurt ourselves or others. *T'shuvah* means turning ourselves around so we can walk on a better path, in a better direction. In order to do this, we need to repair whatever can be repaired, apologize to the people we hurt, and change our hurtful behavior. *T'shuvah* is a big part of Yom Kippur, the Jewish Day of Atonement.

- *Standing at the Edge of the Pit* (page 55)
- *Follow That Goat!* (page 121)
- *Moses Turns Away* (page 149)

TZEDEK · Justice

Many people connect the Hebrew word *tzedakah* with giving charity and helping people, out of the goodness of our hearts. But *tzedek* and *tzedakah* literally mean "justice." The words call us to do the work necessary to make the world more equal and fair. Throughout the Torah, there are rules about making sure that no one has too much or too little and that no one gets special treatment simply because they're rich, famous, or powerful. The Torah tells us, *Tzedek tzedek tirdof*, "Justice, justice, you shall pursue" (Deuteronomy 16:20). Whenever we see a word repeated twice in the Torah, as *tzedek* is here, we know that we really need to pay attention!

- *A Matter of Life and Death* (page 67)
- *Moses Sees* (page 87)
- *Sisters Stand Up for Justice* (page 169)

Discussion Questions

INTRODUCTION · Maybe It Happened This Way

1. Four different kinds of Creation stories are in the introduction—three religious, one scientific. What is your understanding of how the world was created?

2. What does science tell us that the stories in the Torah can't? What do the stories in the Torah tell us that science can't?

3. One of the Creation stories includes the idea that we are responsible for helping God by repairing the world—*tikun olam*. What parts of the world do you think are broken right now? Can you think of any ways, big or small, you might help to fix these problems?

CHAPTER ONE · Adam and Eve Grow Up

1. If you were in Eve's place, would you have eaten the fruit? Why or why not? What if you were in Adam's place?

2. Why do you think the serpent wants Eve to eat the fruit? Why do you think Eve decides to eat the fruit?

3. Have you ever done the right thing for the wrong reasons, or the wrong thing for the right reasons?

CHAPTER TWO · Noah's Hope

1. In Noah's place, would you have been able to keep hoping for better from your neighbors? How do you think Noah is able to do the right thing when those around him behave so badly?

2. Noah's hope for the future is attached to his grandchild. Who or what gives you hope for the future?

3. What do you think the best future for the world would be, and how might you contribute to making that happen?

CHAPTER THREE · Go Forth and Smash the Idols!

1. Have you ever questioned something that the people around you believed to be true? Did you feel like you could share your questions with the people around you?
2. What do you think it means to "be a blessing"?
3. What are some ways that you can be a blessing in the world we live in today?

CHAPTER FOUR · Rebecca Goes Forth

1. The Torah is full of stories of siblings who are favored or not favored. Can you think of a time when you felt that someone in your family got special treatment? How did that make you feel?
2. Do you think there were any other options available to Rebecca in dealing with Laban's behavior, other than leaving her house completely?
3. What would you tell a friend who was dealing with a bully like Laban?

CHAPTER FIVE · Sisters Stick Together

1. When have you stepped in or stepped up to prevent bullying? When have you wished you could have stood up to a bully?
2. How do you feel about Rachel and Jacob tricking Laban to help Leah? Can you think of other ways that they might have made everyone's lives better?
3. What are some ways that you can help people who are being bullied?

CHAPTER SIX · Standing at the Edge of the Pit

1. What do you think made it so difficult for Joseph and his brothers to get along? What do you think each of the characters—Jacob, Joseph, or his brothers—could have done differently to make their relationship better?

2. If you were Joseph, do you think you would have been able to forgive your brothers? Why or why not?

3. When have you been jealous of a family member or a friend? How did being jealous make you act differently toward that person? What might you have done differently to build a better relationship with them?

CHAPTER SEVEN · A Matter of Life and Death

1. How did the midwives decide what to do when faced with Pharaoh's command? What guided them in making that decision?

2. What guides you when you have to make a difficult decision? How do you decide what voices to listen to?

3. Shifra's and Puah's actions are what some people call "civil disobedience," which means disobeying a law that you believe to be unfair. What other stories of civil disobedience have you learned about?

CHAPTER EIGHT · Miriam Saves Her Brother

1. Who are the people in charge around you? What can you do if you think someone in charge is not doing the right thing?

2. Why do some people (like the soldiers in this story) follow orders that they know are wrong, while others (like Miriam, Yocheved, and Pharaoh's daughter) find ways to get around them? What would make you choose to obey or disobey such an order?

CHAPTER NINE · Moses Sees

1. Have you ever had to do something that you didn't feel ready to do? How did you handle it? What and whom did you need to help you?

2. Moses was once a prince, used to luxury; then he became a shepherd, which involved sleeping in the dirt and following around a bunch of sheep. But Moses was happy as a shepherd. What do you think makes something enjoyable? Have you ever been surprised to enjoy something you didn't think you would?

3. This is not the first time that a biblical character talks back to God. What does it say about our people that we argue with and disagree with God?

CHAPTER TEN · Dancing on the Shores of the Sea

1. Why do you think it was so important for the women in Egypt to make music and to dance, even while they were slaves?
2. What gives you hope when you feel hopeless? What are the songs, stories, or activities that lift your spirits when you feel down?
3. Have you ever witnessed something that you believed to be a miracle? What did you do to celebrate what you saw?

CHAPTER ELEVEN · Standing, Sitting, and Signing at Sinai

1. What does it mean to be created *b'tzelem Elohim*? How might we explain the idea that every human being is created in the image of God, when we are all so different?
2. Have you ever felt excluded from something because you were different? How did that feel? What could other people have done to make you feel included and welcome?
3. Have you ever participated in something that left other people out? What could you do instead to make them feel included and welcome?

CHAPTER TWELVE · (Don't) Give Up Your Gold!

1. Can you remember a time when you had to wait a long time for something? How did you feel? Was there anything you could do to help yourself be more patient?
2. Think of something that belongs to you that you would never give away. Why is it so important to you?
3. What is something important that you might help build in your community? What gifts can you give—physical or spiritual—to your community?

CHAPTER THIRTEEN · Follow That Goat!

1. Can you think of something you have done that you later regretted? How did you try to make things right? What might you do differently next time?

2. Think about the times when you have "stumbled" or gotten "stuck," like Tzvi or like the goat. How did you get unstuck? When have people helped you, and when have you done it yourself?

CHAPTER FOURTEEN · Please, God, Heal Her

1. How does Aaron learn to show more kindness to people who are sick? What are some ways that you can show kindness to people who are sick, hurt, or sad?

2. People who had *tzara'at* had to spend time away from the community, which must have been lonely, sad, or even scary. Are there people or groups of people who might feel isolated in our own communities? How can we help them feel less lonely, sad, or scared?

CHAPTER FIFTEEN · Seeing through Caleb Eyes

1. Why do you think it is so hard for the Israelites to believe Caleb's good report? Why do you think it is often easier for people to believe bad news than good news?

2. When might it be important to "look at the bright side"? Why might it be important to consider the downside as well?

3. Think of some instances when you've been able to shift your perspective from the negative to the positive. What helped you to see things in a better light?

CHAPTER SIXTEEN · Moses Turns Away

1. The story of Moses being kept from entering the Promised Land is usually interpreted as a punishment, perhaps one overly harsh. Here, it's more of a gift—a relief from burden. Have you ever been told you can't do something, and secretly (or not so secretly) you've been relieved? Are there any "privileges" in your life that you actually find scary or difficult? What are they?

2. Moses has, for most of his adult life, tried to do the very best, most righteous thing—but he has occasionally lost his temper, as he does now getting water from the rock. Do you find it difficult to do what you know is the right thing in the moment? What helps you keep control of your temper in difficult situations?

CHAPTER SEVENTEEN · Why Curse When You Can Bless?

1. Have you ever had to tell someone something that they didn't want to hear? When have you had to say something that you knew would be unpopular? How did you summon the courage to speak the truth?

2. In this story, a donkey sees what's going on before any of the humans do. What does this tell you about the humans in the story? Have you ever had trouble noticing something that was right in front of you?

3. When Balaam finally looks at the Israelites on his own, he is surprised by what he sees. Take a moment to think about your own community. What makes it special? What are its blessings?

CHAPTER EIGHTEEN · Sisters Stand Up for Justice

1. Have you ever encountered a rule that you didn't think was fair? What did you say? What did you do?

2. Can you think of some times in history or in your own lifetime when people stood up or spoke out because something wasn't fair? What did they do to try to make change happen?

3. Think of some people you could work with to make change happen. Why did you choose them, and what might you do to stand up for justice together?

CHAPTER NINETEEN · The Remembering Song

1. How do you remember the things that are most important to you?

2. If you were going to write a song to remember what was most important to you, your family, or your community, what would you include?

CHAPTER TWENTY · The Crowns on the Letters

1. Think of something important you learned from someone who came before you. From whom did you learn it, and why is it important?

2. What is something important that you'd like to teach to the next generation? How will you make sure that this teaching gets passed along?

3. What questions do you have today that the generations before you would not have thought to ask? Ask some of the adults in your life how the world has changed since they were your age.

Index of Values and Sources

INTRODUCTION · Maybe It Happened This Way 1
   (Genesis 1–2; Rabbi Isaac Luria)
      · *B'tzelem Elohim* (In the Image of God)
      · *Emet* (Truth)

CHAPTER ONE · Adam and Eve Grow Up 5
   (Genesis 2–3)
      · *Emet* (Truth)

CHAPTER TWO · Noah's Hope 17
   (Genesis 6:9–9:17; *Tanchuma Noach* 5:6)
      · *Tikvah* (Hope)
      · *L'dor Vador* (From Generation to Generation)

CHAPTER THREE · Go Forth and Smash the Idols! 25
   (Genesis 12:1–6; Genesis Rabbah 38:13)
      · *Emet* (Truth)
      · *Emunah* (Faith)

CHAPTER FOUR · Rebecca Goes Forth 33
   (Genesis 24)
      · *Sh'lom Bayit* (Peace in the Home)
      · *Chesed* (Kindness)

CHAPTER FIVE · Sisters Stick Together 47
   (Genesis 29–31; Babylonian Talmud, *Megillah* 13b)
      · *Sh'lom Bayit* (Peace in the Home)
      · *Chesed* (Kindness)

CHAPTER SIX · Standing at the Edge of the Pit 55
   (Genesis 37–50; Genesis Rabbah 100:8)
      · *Sh'lom Bayit* (Peace in the Home)
      · *T'shuvah* (Fixing Our Mistakes)

CHAPTER SEVEN · A Matter of Life and Death 67
   (Exodus 1:15–22)
     · *B'tzelem Elohim* (In the Image of God)
     · *Ometz Leiv* (Courage)
     · *Pikuach Nefesh* (Saving a Life)
     · *Tzedek* (Justice)

CHAPTER EIGHT · Miriam Saves Her Brother 75
   (Exodus 2:1–10)
     · *Ometz Leiv* (Courage)
     · *Pikuach Nefesh* (Saving a Life)

CHAPTER NINE · Moses Sees 87
   (Exodus 3)
     · *Tzedek* (Justice)

CHAPTER TEN · Dancing on the Shores of the Sea 95
   (Exodus 14:5–15:20; *M'chilta d'Rabbi Yishmael* 15:20:2)
     · *Tikvah* (Hope)
     · *Emunah* (Faith)
     · *Hidur Mitzvah* (Making Our Traditions Beautiful)

CHAPTER ELEVEN · Standing, Sitting, and Signing at Sinai 103
   (Exodus 19–20; modern midrashim by Matan Koch and Gabrielle Kaplan-Meyer)
     · *B'tzelem Elohim* (In the Image of God)
     · *K'hilah K'doshah* (Sacred Community)

CHAPTER TWELVE · (Don't) Give Up Your Gold! 111
   (Exodus 11:1–2; Exodus 32–36; *Pirkei d'Rabbi Eliezer* 45; Rashi and Ibn Ezra on Exodus 38:8)
     · *Hidur Mitzvah* (Making Our Traditions Beautiful)

CHAPTER THIRTEEN · Follow That Goat! 121
   (Leviticus 16; Rashi on Leviticus 16:8)
     · *T'shuvah* (Fixing Our Mistakes)

CHAPTER FOURTEEN · Please, God, Heal Her 129
   (Leviticus 13–14; Numbers 12; Leviticus Rabbah 16:1; Rashi on Numbers 12:1)
     · *Chesed* (Kindness)

CHAPTER FIFTEEN · Seeing through Caleb Eyes 137
   (Numbers 13–14; Exodus Rabbah 24:1; Babylonian Talmud, *Sotah* 34b–35a)
   · *Tikvah* (Hope)
   · *Emunah* (Faith)

CHAPTER SIXTEEN · Moses Turns Away 149
   (Numbers 20:1–13)
   · *T'shuvah* (Fixing Our Mistakes)
   · *K'hilah K'doshah* (Sacred Community)

CHAPTER SEVENTEEN · Why Curse When You Can Bless? 157
   (Numbers 22–24)
   · *K'hilah K'doshah* (Sacred Community)

CHAPTER EIGHTEEN · Sisters Stand Up for Justice 169
   (Numbers 27:1–11, 36:1–13)
   · *Ometz Leiv* (Courage)
   · *Tzedek* (Justice)

CHAPTER NINETEEN · The Remembering Song 177
   (Deuteronomy 31–32)
   · *Ometz Leiv* (Courage)
   · *K'hilah K'doshah* (Sacred Community)
   · *L'dor Vador* (From Generation to Generation)

CHAPTER TWENTY · The Crowns on the Letters 185
   (Babylonian Talmud, *M'nachot* 29b)
   · *Hidur Mitzvah* (Making Our Traditions Beautiful)
   · *L'dor Vador* (From Generation to Generation)

Acknowledgments

First and foremost, we are grateful to our families and friends for their unwavering support and encouragement while we were writing this book. Thank you to Dena Neusner and David Behrman, for embracing our vision for this project, and Leslie Kimmelman, for helping us bring it to fruition. Thank you to our early readers: Heidi Aycock, Allison Ofanansky, and Rachel Margolis. Thank you especially to Matan Koch and Gabrielle Kaplan-Meyer for their help with "Standing, Sitting, and Signing at Sinai," which was inspired by Matan's Shavuot sermon "Standing at Sinai" (May 2015, matankoch.com).

We are grateful to Brandeis University, where we met, and the Yiddish Book Center, for hosting the Jewish Creativity Conference that inspired both of us to be writers and midrashists.

Thank you to all of our writing teachers, especially Jill McCorkle, Alicia Ostriker, Gerald Shapiro *z"l*, Alison Jones, and Carly Husick. And thank you to the following organizations for providing the writing communities that helped us grow and through which much of this book was written: the Yiddish Book Center, PJ Library, the Jewish Studio Project, the Highlights Foundation, Wildacres Writers' Retreat, Resource Center for Women in Ministry in the South, and the Union for Reform Judaism Six Points Creative Arts Academy. We are also grateful to our professors at Hebrew Union College–Jewish Institute of Religion, the University of Illinois Chicago English Department, and the University of Chicago Divinity School.

Thank you to our spiritual communities, past and present, especially our current ones: Congregation Kol Ami in Elkins Park, Pennsylvania, and Or Shalom in Vernon Hills, Illinois. Thank you to all of the Jewish professionals who nudged us to finally write this book so we could have more story collections to share with our communities. Erica would especially like to thank Dale Truding, for giving her the confidence to push forward with this project, and Cara Moroze, who inspired and informed her as a Jewish educator.

Thank you to our students of all ages, especially Tyne Tyson, who, as a bat mitzvah student at Judea Reform Congregation, asked the question that sparked Leah's interest in making the stories of the Torah accessible to inquisitive young minds.

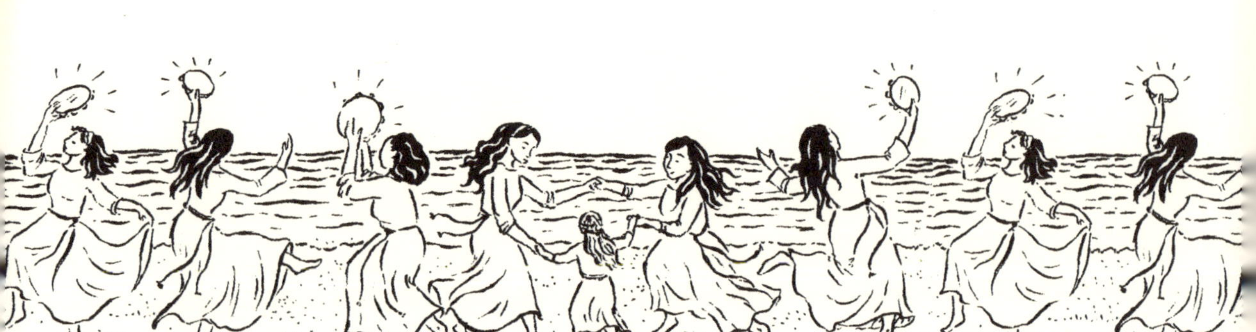